Another Life Again

ISBN No. 0 907011 06 3 Hardback.
ISBN No. 0 907011 05 5 Paperback.

Published 1981 by The Irish Times Ltd.,
© Michael & Ethna Viney
© Drawings by Michael Viney
Distributed by The Irish Times General Services
16 D'Olier St., Dublin 2. Tel. 722022.
Cover design by The Irish Times Studio
Typesetting and artwork PrintSet & Design Ltd., Tel. (01) 724588
Printed in Ireland by E. & T. O'Brien Ltd. Tel. (01) 606333.

Another Life Again

Michael & Ethna Viney

An Irish Times Publication

Introduction

IF YOU READ my first book, *Another Life,* or follow our family chronicle in *The Irish Times* on Saturdays, you will know what to expect from this sequel. The first flood from the mountain is waiting overleaf and you may plunge, so to speak, straight into it. But newcomers will want to know how the story began — and why.

It is now a bit more than four years since we moved from suburban Dublin to an acre of remotest Mayo to shape a happier, healthier life in the most beautiful place we know. Ethna and I were in our mid-forties; our daughter, Michele, was eight. We had sold our city home and resigned from secure, successful jobs in journalism and television. We were seeking the ultimate luxury, the final privilege, of living simply and pleasing ourselves.

There will be times in reading this book when you may wonder if we are serious or honest, if we really enjoy the hard work, the extravagant weather, the menial rural chores. Are we not a bit mad to be getting up at five, even on a January morning?

There must be things we would not do if we were rich, but they do not rush to mind. We would still want to grow our own food, because working with the soil seems to touch some spring of contentment — and because our vegetables *are* the best we ever tasted. We would still want to bake our own bread and make our own wine. We would still want to set the spillet to catch fish on the strand, because it is something we do together, sharing the sunsets and dawns. We might, if pressed, let somebody else foot the turf. But hard work was part of the price of a beautiful environment, of clean air and kindly silence. It was also something we looked forward to. It seemed to us more natural to use brain and body both, day by day. So virtue and necessity coincide.

The "self-sufficient" life is not for everyone. Indeed, in her last word to the book, Ethna dwells on our anti-social conduct in opting out of consumption; if everybody did it, the nation as we know it would collapse! But a great many people, it seems, are pleased to know that it can be made to work and have enjoyed sharing our exploits and even the practical trivia of life on one intensive acre.

From the letters that come to us from readers of *Another Life*, we know that we have touched some very deep emotions, convictions, dissatisfactions with the thrust of urban living. Our improvisations may be clumsy and sometimes absurd, but they do bear witness to the adaptability of ordinary, middle-class city people, whether in hooking a thornback ray or milking a fractious goat. We can all survive.

A word about where we are. If you look at a map of Ireland and find the fiord of Killary Harbour, which separates Galway and Mayo, we live just north of the mouth of the fiord, where the foothills of Mweelrea Mountain slope down to the sea. With our back to the ridge of Six Noggins, we look out across thirty miles of sea and islands to an enormous, ever-changing sky. In this remote corner of Connacht, we have been made welcome by a community which has been doing things the hard way for many generations. A little of what we owe to our neighbours should emerge between the lines of this book.

I tell most of the story, much as it appeared originally in *The Irish Times*. But in the autumn of 1980 I went off on a bicycle journey round Ireland and Ethna was left to take over the chronicle, along with the harvest of barley and potatoes. She has also stepped in at other times, when my labours on the acre have had to come first. Her contributions in this book will add a lively perspective and help to confirm, perhaps, that this really is turning out to be the time of our lives.

Michael Viney

Thallabawn, Killadoon, Co Mayo.
December, 1981.

Contents

A Lump of Rain	9
Coming in Handy	13
Crow to Pluck	17
Mine Own Executioner	21
Time by the Forelock	25
Backing Báinin	29
One Man and His Dog	33
Strange Landmarks	37
Trip to Town	41
Scents of Spring	45
Far-Off Voices	49
Running Low	53
The Hungry Gap	57
Feeling Good	61
Little Luxuries	65
Thelwell Days	69
Keeping the Peace	73
Summer Vintage	77
Birds of Passage	81
Room at the Top	85
Working Arrangements Ethna Viney	89
Minority View "	93
Wild and Free "	97
Goat Games "	101

A Yard of Badger	105
A Two-Fisted Milker	109
Earthworks	113
Along the Tide	117
Staff of Life	119
All Due Modesty	123
Passing the Time	127
The Inheritors	131
Beastly Chores	135
A Bit of a Breeze	139
The Long View	143
The Swing of It	147
Time and Tide	151
Under the Hedge	155
Nightline	159
A Day for Twins	163
Horns of a Dilemma	167
Harbourworks	171
Bridle Path	175
Separate Dreams	179
Pro Bono Publico Ethna Viney	183

A Lump of Rain

ALL MORNING THE wind had come from the mountain, flinging rain so hard against the windows that they wept at the seams. The gale was forecast south-easterly, veering south. But at mid-day came a curious change. The wind died away from Mweelrea and swung right across to the north-west. At the same time the rain intensified, thudding and drumming in a premature dusk. Our weather-wise neighbours said afterwards that they knew it would make a big lump of rain when the wind jumped the sky like that.

There were several days back in the summer when the water rushed off the hill fast enough to make us uneasy. We remembered the Big Flood of five years ago that battered down bridges and swept cattle, sheep and haystacks out to sea. It was a wild, local freak of the mountains, everyone said at the time; it might happen once in a century. But it stayed at the back of the mind. It was why we put the beehives high up in The Hollow and not on the banks of the stream. When I built the fowlhouse on the bank, there were jokes about the ducks being floated out of bed.

At least they were not in bed now. As the flood surged out of the stream, lifting the footbridge of logs and turning The Hollow into a churning maelstrom, ducks and geese retreated to a hillock under the ditch. The birds forgot their territorial squabbles and shrank together in dismay, mesmerised by the pounding rush of water. Their house was soon half submerged and throwing up a bow wave.

The noise of a flood of this kind is unforgettable: there is something in the sound of rocks being smashed and ground together that stirs primeval alarm. As the torrents from the hill converged at the road bridge and leaped through its arch into The Hollow, their hidden weight of stones and boulders were swept down over the waterfall in an echoing cannonade. Along at Tommy Joe's, where the river curves down from the mountain, the sound was "like houses falling" and the road bridge trembled from the passage of the rocks. Cattle ran up from the river banks, lowing in fear, and were given hay to calm them.

For almost two hours, we alternated between frantic activity out in the rain and sodden contemplation through the window. In our sorties outside, we were snatching up lumber from the path of the flood or deepening the trench that might keep the water from the shed. At the window, we awaited lesser or greater disasters. In another foot or two, the flood would reach the bees. If the willow tree broke loose and wedged across the ditch, the water would rise in seconds and tear even bigger lumps from the bank beside the house. Or the road bridge might go.

When it became apparent that none of these would happen, we had time to wonder how Báinin was getting on. The field he was grazing was bounded on three sides by the mountain river where it made its last curve to the strand. The whole of the this low-lying "delta" area was now awash, all boundaries confused. As the rain eased, I set off in thighboots down a boreen scoured to its foundations. I met Michael, our neighbour, who warned me not to let myself be seen by the pony, or by any of the cattle stranded with him across the river. They might try to swim to me and be swept away.

Where the boreen disappeared finally under water, I took to the fields and dodged along a ridge of hillocks to a place where I could crouch with binoculars. Báinin stood on an island, behind a little field-byre crammed with cows. His silver hide was black with rain. He's a tough moorland pony, we tell ourselves; we shouldn't fuss.

As the last of the flood emptied into the sea, staining it brown in an arc across the bay, its legacy in debris and devastated fencing was revealed. In the glen behind Joe's house, the river had swept across a fertile meadow, leaving a great beach of rocks and gravel fifty yards across. Our neighbours are usually philosophical about flood damage — "Ah, it'll keep me busy during the winter" — but to lose three good acres under a moraine of stones is a blow by any standards.

Among the flattened fences was the one at the end of Báinin's field, so we went next morning to bring him back up the hill. He had strayed out on the strand, to join other loose horses, but came gladly enough to be bridled. Rather than risk him balking at unfamiliar obstacles — deep pools on the road, banks of silt, trailing wires — Ethna led him at full tilt, jumping and plunging. But he seemed only too pleased to be leaving such an untrustworthy landscape.

All kinds of livestock were behaving a little strangely, as if suffering from shock. One of Michael's cows was balancing absurdly on a narrow ditch, even though the ground around was dry. A farm dog that usually ambushes me cringed to the hedge as if terrified. Our geese and ducks refused to leave the fowlhouse to face their ravaged stream and, when at last persuaded, ignored their morning basins of feed.

There was a day's work for me in The Hollow, chopping away the torn banks of the stream and heaving boulders about to leave a clear flow. Austie came by to lean on the bridge and advise: "You'll want to chop those rushes back or it'll take your little shedeen." My little shedeen — the fowlhouse — had actually survived very well, with only a few inches of silt to show for its inundation. It's our housheen I worry about, as the erosion of the high banks creeps nearer to its foundations. But though the flood did break away another couple of feet, it also gouged the bed of the stream to twice its former depth, so that the normal flow is now a safe babble at the bottom of a canyon.

The most urgent job in the wake of the flood was to restore our water supply. Like most of our neighbours, we had installed water by running a one-inch plastic pipe up the hillside to a point in the stream well above the level of our roof, fitting a filter to the end and wedging it to lie submerged in a pool. This brings the water down by gravity, sometimes with great force or coloured to a deep, boggy brown which, in the bath, in certain lights, has the glint of goldfish in its depths.

The flood interrupted our water supply by abolishing the pool, so that the end of the pipe was left suspended in mid-air. With advice from Michael, who had been similarly disconnected, I set about relaying the pipe. The skill is in dealing with the air that is trapped in the system when the flow resumes — a problem to be dealt with by primitive physics and a fine judgment of bubbles. How much more fun than waiting for the Corporation!

Coming in Handy

IN DUBLIN WE had an attic; here we have a shed. When Michael and Paddy were helping to build it, adding to the ruin of the old stone cart house at the gate, they called it a barn, reluctant to think that anyone could want a building that big just to fill with things that might come in handy one day. They reckoned without the middle-class urban detritus that could produce, say twenty half-empty cans of paint, all of different colours, or four blunt pairs of hedge-clippers and a defunct motor-mower.

Without going out of our way to buy in junk (an exception were the three big wine casks, at a fiver each, which have found invaluable uses), we gathered up materials for our move like a Swiss Family Robinson tipped off about the shipwreck. Every off-cut of timber from my spasms of carpentry, every screw, bolt and washer, every metal thingamajig made the trip across Ireland. We stored up all kinds of containers, against the day when we would stop buying processed foods. We needed jars by the score for the summer, yet to come, when the bees produce a proper honey surplus. We accumulated egg cartons, wine bottles, yoghurt tubs and anything with a lid.

Unlike the attic, embalmed in dust and mouse-droppings, the shed has been organic in our lives, digesting wave after wave of activity. Three or four times a year, when the last space for the bicycle has silted up with plastic sacks, I mount a major reorganisation. This week, the need was even more pressing than usual. We had decided to make a stable in one end of the shed, so that we can bring Báinın in from the hillside on bad winter nights.

Excavating the contents, layer by layer, I thought again of Henry Thoreau and his exhortation to simplicity. To achieve a rural life which many would call "simple", we have already had to master quite a complicated set of skills. And the shed's recesses yielded reminders of yet more projects unfulfilled. This old gramophone turntable is to carry a potter's wheel, so that we can experiment with the clay at the bottom of Joe's meadow. This net, like a giant's Christmas stocking, is to trap the river eels, if there are any. These anchors are to use on the long line, if we ever have the mackerel for bait.

Like many barns along the Western seaboard, ours is now festooned with beachcomber's booty. In particular, there are buoys of every size, from the bright little baubles used as markers, to the weightier trawlerballs of the Danes and Norwegians, to the big, robust balloons — blandies, as the Kerrymen call them — whose pink fluorescence can be spotted half a-mile away. The latest of these, brightening the whole shed with its pink party glow, came ashore trailing twenty fathoms of rope.

None of my neighbours has much use for buoys; their first hope from beachcombing is nets, especially now that synthetic fibres have given them such long lives. I have a torn stretch of net holding down the rushes on our rick of turf, but many farmers this side of the hill have sections of net ten times the size and covering whole haystacks.

Really big timber is rare enough, but everything over a couple of feet long is hauled above the tideline, or marked with stones or a piece of rope to show it has been found. Without a tractor to carry it home, I cannot compete for the timber that would make good winter logs.

At a mariculture seminar across in Clifden recently, a spokesman for the inshore fishermen described our bays and estuaries as "a continuing source of washed-in wealth", to be set alongside the harvesting of seaweed or the taking of sand and gravel. This would have surprised many people who do not know the coastal economy. Compared with the rich jetsam of World War Two, most of what comes ashore today is intrinsically trivial; it is use that gives value. I am pleased, for example, to find a wooden fish box in which to raise seedlings, or a plastic milk crate in which to store vegetables.

It is a strange thing, but true, that I have yet to meet any of my neighbours beachcombing: I am always alone on the strand. And yet, unless I am abroad at first light, there are always footprints ahead of mine. An islander friend has told me that the secret of successful beachcoming, as of so much else, is simple perseverance. "If people know that you always walk the shore at dawn, they will stay in bed on the bad mornings and leave it to you." But I do not want exclusive rights — just the pleasure, now and then, of being first.

One morning last week, with the house shuddering to the gusts of a westerly gale, I decided to walk the tideline to see if it helps to be there, so to speak, at the point of delivery. Leaning into the wind, with a hand cupped to my face to let me keep my eyes open, I found the breakers piled high into foaming terraces and lumps of froth being whisked ashore to fetch up, quivering, against the dunes.

But after all that, it was an empty sea. My only trophy was a helmet from an oil rig, drilling somewhere out there above the Porcupine Bank in unimaginable waves. The helmet is the first sign of things to come — but not, I hope, more than we bargain for. At the height of the North Sea oil rush, the rigs were a notorious source of debris, much of it costly material, lost overboard or extravagantly discarded. Some of it came ashore; more of it was caught in fishing nets, which it damaged or tainted with oil.

The helmet — the kind proof against monkey-wrenches dropped from a height — was very welcome. It will do as a riding hat for Ethna, and, painted black, should look almost as smart as her daughter's.

Making a stable for Báinín was not just a simple matter of clearing one end of the shed and putting up a timber partition. The floor slopes inwards from the doors next to the road, as we found to our cost in last month's flood. And a healthy pony pisses copiously. If the lower end of the shed (where, along with everything else, we store the potatoes) was not to become unduly noisome, the area of the stable would have to be raised and sloped outwards. Even with a foundation of broken blocks and gravel, I had to mix and spread the best part of a ton of concrete, which is the hardest kind of work I know.

It made me appreciate even more the skill of the horsemen of East Anglian farms, who used to train their horses to piss before entering their stables at night, on the cue of a whistle. Inquiring of my neighbours how such training might be achieved, they can suggest only that I . . . er . . . tickle Báinín while whistling an appropriate note. But even if he takes in good part this attempt at equine potty training, it sounds too much like something you could be had up for.

Crow to Pluck

IT DIDN'T SEEM such a bad gale at the time: a stiff blow from the sea in mid-August that leaned on us for half a day and left our field of vegetables a bit bowed down but not, we thought, actually broken. I had almost forgotten it when, a week or so later, the long ridges of potatoes began suddenly to blacken and wilt.

So rapid was their transformation that Michael came over the ditch to wonder if we had blight. "It can't be." I insisted. "I've sprayed four times already." But if it was the wind, why were Michael's ridges, high on the hill and quite without shelter, still green and flourishing?

I found a photograph of blight, in a book, to reassure myself that the blotches on the leaves were wind-bruises and not the leprosy of *Phytophthora infestans*. But it was not until the first potatoes were lifted and found healthy that I really stopped feeling uneasy. A half-matured crop was bad enough; a blighted one is worse than none at all.

So what I have learned is that, in some gales, the thorn-topped ditches down two sides of our field actually trap and funnel the wind and increase its turbulence. On the open hillside, it is free to run and flow. I think of the naturalist Fraser Darling, when he farmed an island in the Hebrides, going out in storms to stand with the plants at various corners of his land to see how it felt to grow there.

Now, as I fork my way down the ridges in a late harvesting, the gale has left its print on the crop. From the size and number of potatoes per plant, I can track it exactly. Only the plants crouched under the ditch or knocked sprawling in the furrows lived out their natural span. The rest withered prematurely, most of their potatoes not much bigger than the seed they grew from, so that I am unlikely to reach one ton in a year that might have given me two.

All I can do about the summer gales is break their force with hedging and fencing. But it is pretty much my own fault that, in harvesting the potatoes, I am having to race against the crows.
It was sheer smugness that made me leave the crop in the ridges and press on with other work, while Michael had his potatoes lifted and clamped before the end of October. I knew that, unlike most of my neighbours, I had given the ridges a good thick covering of soil; the

cultivator makes a much easier job of earthing-up. When the crows came spud-hunting, as they do every autumn, they would go first to the fields where potatoes were bulging up through the soil, and leave my anonymous earth-works alone.

But I had reckoned without the "lumps" of rain that fell at the start of November and the diligent cunning of the rook and jackdaw. The rain hammered the soil off the shoulders of the ridges, exposing the outermost Records to view. Once the birds knew what was under the soil, they went digging. When I went down the ridges at the end of the wet spell, they were strewn with excavated tubers.

No one begrudges the crows the tiny *po-eens* left from harvesting (though even these we would rather feed to the hens), but these unholy crows seem to have an instinct that guides them to the best of the crop. And just as seals and otters are reputed to take one bite of a salmon before going on to tackle another, the jackdaw takes a few pecks from a potato — just enough to spoil it for storage — before digging out the next. At the first, dismayed inspection, I gathered up a hundredweight.

Even Michael, for all his prudence, has suffered from the crows' wanton pilferage. He covered his clamp of potatoes with rushes and put fishing net over that to hold the thatch in place. But the birds incredibly, managed to extract two bucketfuls of tubers through the meshes.

The rooks live in the only proper clump of trees for miles. Most of the farms this side of the hill have some sort of shelter belt of pines, but only one, a two-storey house just down the hill from us, has a copse of dark sycamores enfolding it, like elms around a rectory. Three years ago, the man of the house was killed in a tractor accident. He was an energetic farmer, who always found time to keep down the number of rooks nesting in his trees (not least because of the racket they created outside his bedroom window) by using his shotgun or breaking up the nests in spring.

This control was interrupted in the year before we came. And our arrival made matters worse by adding a new and convenient source of food — not only more potatoes, but an extra crop of barley and profligate basins of poultry food. The rooks have multiplied tenfold.

What is needed, it might seem, is something like the old rook-shoots of gamekeepers' England. On each May 12th, the squire would muster a house-party of guests to surround the rookery, in full shooting-dress, and direct a barrage of fire into the treetops. A fair score on such a day might be five hundred birds, which the guests would take away in bunches after a buffet at the Hall. Rook pie, according to a recipe I have, demanded newly-fledged birds with their backs removed and baked with beefsteak, rashers and hard-boiled eggs and plenty of black pepper.

Fledgling jackdaw might need even more pepper, but the present price of cartridges would rule out even a modest massacre by shotgun. Poisoned grain would be too indiscriminate and birdlime uncertain and messy (birdlime, as still used — illegally — by some British finch-trappers, is a sticky decoction of holly twigs, linseed and barley, boiled down for a day).

You will recognise all these threats as bloodthirsty fantasy, contrived as I labour at the ridges (spearing almost as many potatoes with my fork as the crows do with their beaks).

Digging there the other morning — one of the quiet, golden days in whch autumn, for all my talk of floods and gales, has excelled — I heard a noise from across the ditch as if someone were driving stakes with a sledgehammer. There would be half a minute's silence and then *thock!* an echoing concussion.

In the field beyond, two rams were fighting — one of them, perhaps, without much choice. He had charged at his opponent through a wire fence and got his great curved horns entangled in it. The other ram was now taking his time, backing off a few yards before launching himself into the battering collision of skulls. Between impacts, the two animals nuzzled each other in what could have passed for affection, and drew dreamy lines on the turf with their delicate hoofs. Perhaps they were dazed.

November is the month for running the rams with the ewes and there will be many such fights among those left to roam the hill. They can keep up their head-to-head charges for as long as two hours, and a ram can lose a horn in the battle, or even be killed. More often, a quick tussle will end in surrender, so that one ram will never challenge his victor again.

Uncertain how to separate the rams next door, I called on Michael, who simply unhooked the wire from the trapped contestant and let him run away.

Mine Own Executioner

HOW LONG IS it since you killed anything? Not a wasp or a trespassing spider, I mean, but something that struggled and bled all over the place? In what is called a violent age, most people lead lives of fastidious gentleness, especially if they live in cities and buy their meat in plastic bags. How many Dubliners could kill their own Christmas turkey?

On this side of the hill, miles from a butcher's shop, most farmers' wives despatch their poultry as a matter of course. But not every farmer, by any means, will kill his own bullock or sheep, even if he has a freezer, and the man with a ready nerve for it will be in demand by his neighbours.

When we were rebuilding the cart house at the gate, I found an iron ring set into a slab in the floor. I supposed, romantically, that the slab was meant to be lifted — but a pickaxe found nothing but earth underneath. In fact, the ring was to help in slaughtering: a tether from the beast would be run through the ring and its head pulled down for the stunning.

In our first year here, before we grew so many vegetables, we bought lambs for the freezer. In the beginning, they were killed for us and the finished carcasses handed over for hanging and cutting up. But as our lives grew closer to those of our neighbours I was inevitably drawn into helping with the killing. Wasn't I, after all, the self-sufficient man, interested in how everything was done? The least I could do was to hold the sheep still while the blade was being used.

In Connacht — and, for all I know, generally in sheep-farming Ireland — a lamb is killed in what I used to think of as the *kosher* way: a vein is cut in the neck and the animal bled to death. Until my initiation, I had no idea what to expect, but I took it for granted the sheep would be stunned in some way. In fact, it's not, and the couple of minutes it takes to lie still can seem very long.

By the time that the jump in lamb prices made them too costly to buy, even from our neighbours, I found it no hardship at all to stop eating meat every day and settle for our own fresh vegetables. While there had been a certain technical interest in the preparation of a carcass, and I had learned how to skin with my fist, the actual execution was getting no easier to take. On one occasion, I was offered the knife and invited to try my hand, but I knew that I never could.

Meanwhile, our poultry were multiplying and falling due for the freezer. Ethna, for all her rural background, was not volunteering (though she had, in her time, killed chickens by slamming a door on their necks). I knew that one "wrung" a chicken's neck, but what precisely did this mean? The books described how you grip and push and twist; it has nothing in common with wringing a dishcloth.

The books also brought home the fact that geese and ducks, being bigger, have tougher necks. In the method suggested for them, the neck is dislocated by resting the bird's chin on the ground, placing a stout bar across the back of its neck, putting a foot on each end of the bar and then pulling the bird upwards. I have bungled this too often now to recommend it.

I was determined from the start that we should not be undone by sentiment. There were not to be cries of "I really can't eat poor Josephine!" But ducks, in particular, seem equipped with all the quirks of stance, expression and behaviour that amuse, and seduce the affections. They do not even need names, or special attention, to make their deaths upsetting.

By the time our first ducklings hatched out, late in the summer, I made a conscious effort to keep my distance. These birds were bred for the table, not as pets. At ten weeks precisely, when their food conversion rate had reached its peak, the kitchen was cleared to receive five birds for plucking.

Ten-week Aylesburys are almost adult in size, but they are tender enough to have their necks wrung. I seized the first bird and wrapped an arm round its silky white wings and knew without a doubt that this was murder. It was made so beautifully, it had lived so short a time! Closing down my feelings, I pushed and twisted, and grabbed and pushed and twisted four times more. The row of corpses on the kitchen floor shone like crumpled damask. We plucked in mutual misery, and by the last feather had come to a decison: we will breed ducks for their eggs but never again for ten-week "processing".

By November, the remaining geese were also due for killing. They were not of a good enough breed to carry through the winter and were gobbling food every day without gaining an extra ounce. Yet time kept slipping by. "We must start killing the geese on Monday," Ethna would say. "Yes, we must," I'd agree.

We finally came to it last week. With the first goose, I once again tried the bar across the neck and once again the skin tore and the neck refused to break. I could have wept with frustration and self disgust. Next morning, for the last two geese, I assembled a hatchet, a plank and a pail of water. It was messy, but quickest of all.

Left in possession of The Hollow, the adult ducks and Fred, the drake, fell strangely silent and ignored their food. The geese had bossed and bullied them all year — sometimes so severely that we had rushed to separate them. But now, instead of celebrating the end of their daily harassment, the ducks roamed The Hollow as if at a loose end. They missed the company of their tormentors.

I have tried to sort out what I feel about killing for food. To be squeamish, says the dictionary, is to be "easily nauseated, fastidious, overnice, overscrupulous" — so whatever I am, it isn't that. "I really don't mind killing things." I used to tell Ethna, "so long as I can do it cleanly." The sub-Hemingway glibness of this disappeared at the death of the ducklings: they died in a thoroughly competent way, but that made me feel no better.

It isn't even, as once it seemed to be, a mere matter of aesthetics: by this time, blood and guts don't worry me at all so long as they're not mine. No: it has much more to do with destruction — with the wantonness of killing, which is felt so acutely in the middle of doing-it-yourself. We shall insist on enjoying our goose next week, but still not feel at all sure it was worth it.

Time by the Forelock

STARTING RTE'S RADIO programme at 6.30 a.m. has been official recognition that the Irish are getting up earlier. The trend is most apparent in the cities, where the rush-hour advances perceptibly year by year, but it is taking hold, too, in the small towns with new industries and in the rural hinterlands that provide commuting workers. To drive around Clew Bay to Westport in the early morning is to see lighted windows gleaming in the hills and to find people moving in the streets of the town by half-past seven, ahead even of the holy ladies shivering off to Mass.

Patterns of rising are also changing on this side of the hill. Several of the young men are up at six to share cars to jobs in Westport or beyond. Nursing daughters, in cars of their own, head off well before dawn to the hospital in Castlebar. But the big catalyst for change has been free secondary education and the morning discipline of school transport. The minibus for Louisburgh's co-educational convent is waiting at the end of the boreen by eight o'clock, and the bus for the national school is there an hour later.

On a dry-stock farm with sheep on the hill, there is no pressing need to get up on winter mornings, if one can turn a deaf ear to the cattle lowing in the barn. But farmers who bestir themselves with the rest of the family are often quietly gratified by what they can get done. It is in these days of the Christmas school holiday, when the morning road is silent and scarcely a wisp from a chimney is seen before 10, that one senses the slower pulse of the past. In the houses of the sad bachelors, of course, it lingers still, and the porch light from the night before may still be burning wanly at noon.

Bedtimes in Connacht are notoriously late. In summer, farm work often continues until sunset, and even in winter, visiting between neighbours begins at nine or ten. Earlier this month, the traders of Louisburgh got together to agree to close their shops by nine o'clock. The warm light spilling out across the streets on winter nights has given the little towns of the West a special intimacy, but the few late pounds of profit no longer seem worth the vigil.

There are people naturally attuned to the night, but I am not one of them. The Mediterranean holidays of my youth were full of frustration, since nothing romantic or wicked began before midnight, when I was too drowsy to care. By a fortunate chance (since a metabolic mis-match can be disastrous in a marriage), Ethna has much the same energy-cycle. For all her boasts of staying up half the night in Killala, playing poker with cattle-dealers, she shows no more desire than I to join the West's insomniac sessions of Twenty Five.

Indeed, on most nights now we are both asleep by 10 o'clock, having given our lifestyle yet another defiant twist: we are up in the morning at five.

The great freedom of the self-supporting rural life is one's new control over time. If the number of tasks to be done in the day is sometimes overwhelming, at least you can decide what you want to do from one hour to the next. But the conditioning of organised employment can run deep, with persistent rhythms and expectations of the clock.

After so many years of dividing time into blocks of work and leisure, it can be hard to accept and enjoy their intermingling in a self-directed day. Even where modified by managerial "flexitime", urban jobs dictate, as a rule, that work fills the morning and afternoon and leisure the evening. Although our activities had so profoundly changed, we were slow to question this conventional rhythm of work, play and sleep.

When we started homesteading, there were those with experience to warn us that any intellectual activity would have to be tackled first in the day: if we left it until evening, we would be too tired even to write a letter. And so it proved. Even when we tried to hoard energy through the day, we would inevitably be seduced into one outdoor, physical job too many.

It may have been greedy to want more from the 24 hours. But I had promised myself the champagne of dewy summer mornings, and here I was instead, like most of my neighbours, collapsing in front of television by late evening and wrenching myself out of bed next day with the sun already high. Even as the days drew in again, Ethna and I found ourselves starting and ending earlier, but still with no margin of energy for our creative projects.

Each of us, every now and then, had got up at five or thereabouts to finish a piece of writing under pressure of deadline. At that hushed hour, we had been pleasantly surprised to find how alert, productive and cheerful we felt, and how much we could get done before breakfast. As winter deepened, Ethna was slipping out of bed at five more and more often, leaving me to sleep on. But this had its effect at the other end of the day, when I would find myself alone at the fire. If only to put our lives back into synchrony, it seemed a good idea for the Vineys to retire and rise together.

At the end of a month of the new regime, I must report that it works very well. By rearranging the day, we have won back three hours that used to be spent, in passive and grudging somnolence, before the television set. No longer do we have to ask each other: "Why are we watching this rubbish?" And because they are "new" hours, left blank in the reckoning of the nine - to - five world, it does not stir up too much guilt to fill them with unlicensed pursuits.

By the spring, if all goes well, it will have become a habit to start the day with three free hours, so that I can roam forth into the dawn with an easel or a fishing rod and a clear conscience. And if I should find myself hoeing my beans at five, like Henry Thoreau, I shall firmly remind myself that he stopped hoeing his beans at 12 and took the rest of the day off. Despite some appearances, Ethna and I are not a pair of ascetics — just ordinary, guilt-driven hedonists trying to take time by the forelock.

Backing Báinin

ON THOSE RARE occasions when Ethna feels that events may be slipping a little from her control, she dreams that she is driving a double-decker bus — from upstairs. What this might feel like in reality she never expected to discover until, one bracing morning last week, she decided it was time that somebody got up on Báinin.

The last time she sat on a horse, she was 10 years old. On the farm at Glangevlin, she and her br hers would take ilBáinin.

The last time she sat on a horse, she was 10 years old. On the farm at Glangevlin, she and her brothers would take illicit rides on Charlie, a work pony of uncertain temper, given to backing carts into walls. That was 35 years ago, in which time there were no more horses until we bought Báinin.

Even using the patient ways of modern pony training, rather than the brusque confrontations by which most countrymen still "break" a horse, it need not take nine months to bring a two-year-old Connemara colt to the point of accepting a rider. But given our total inexperience, and a year in which every dry day presented more pressing tasks, we feel we have not done too badly.

Báinin's breeder was a woman, so that Ethna's early overtures met with more response than my own. And since she is more patient and dogged by nature, we decided that she should be the trainer. Her one disadvantage was her size: at 5′ 2″, her shoulders and Báinin's withers were roughly on a level. A toss of his head could put it effectively out of her reach, and without a man's weight it was difficult not to let the pony feel his own strength in the tussles over tackling and obeying words of command. She had to succeed by coaxing and tact and endless repetition.

As the work of spring and summer began to crowd our days, there were long intervals when our only contact with the pony was in delivering his evening bucket of nuts. There were only a couple of fistfuls mixed in with the bran, but it kept him pleased to see us and made an occasion for the petting and handling that we knew were so important. The bucket has often been my job, particularly in rough

One Man and his Dog

ANYONE WHO HAS watched the British Sheepdog Trials on television and marvelled at the rapport between the farmer and his collie might feel a little disappointed with the way things are done along Six Noggins. In place of mellifluous whistles to turn the dog this way or that, or send him off to round up a straggler, the mountain air is rent by guttural shouts and curses as collies herd the sheep with much the same indiscriminate enthusiasm as they use in chasing cars. Instead of the control and precision on display for the cameras beside Lake Windermere, most of the herding on this side of the hill proceeds by a series of approximations converging, more or less, on success.

One calm and frosty day last week, with the ravens flapping black against the snow on Mweelrea, I kept young Paddy company on a trip up Six Noggins to find his ewes and bring them to the warmer side of the ridge. With him, as always, was Prince, the collie he was given as a pup nine years ago. As we mounted the ridge, skidding on the boggy slope and crunching through an occasional platter of ice, I asked Paddy how he had trained the dog. "I didn't", he said. "He trained himself".

Never, that is, had Paddy set out to teach Prince to obey specific commands. Rather, the dog's inborn urge to chase and herd was shaped in daily practice: some things were all right to do, others brought roars of disapproval. Routine movements of cattle and sheep taught the collie to anticipate and improvise: "He knows what has to be done". But while such a passive kind of training works well enough on familiar ground, it would probably leave the dog bewildered in the setting of a sheepdog trial, working with strange sheep over new terrain. It is here that specific training, using whistled cues, comes into its own.

The man who can command by whistles can send his dog further and save himself a lot of walking — but only when he knows that those white dots on the hillside are his. On the congested mountain commonages of the West, the sheep in one square mile may belong to half-a-dozen different owners, so that a farmer who wants to gather his own flock needs to be close enough to see their marks — and this means going up beside his dog.

Paddy's ewes are marked fore and aft with blue hoops across the back, painted on with dye after dipping and shearing. We came upon them, grazing in bunches, at the eastern edge of the ridge, where the bog sweeps across under Mweelrea to Doo Lough and the Sheeffrys. When the first great flocks of Blackface were brought in by the Scottish tenant ranchers in the 1850s, this area carried some 50,000 sheep. Young Paddy, with his 50 ewes, lives beside us in a townland that was cleared to make way for the ranchers' stock. "The blackheads and the kyloes our homes and valleys fill," runs an old protest ballad (the kyloes were the ranchers' cattle.)

Paddy may believe that he has never trained his dog, but he communicates constantly with Prince once the dog begins to work. These are orders to "Come up!" or "Go out!", differing inflections on his name and gestures to send him left or right. He likes to hold the dog well out from the sheep, so that they close together gently and move without stampeding.

From what Paddy has seen of the sheepdog trials on television, the dogs do too much rushing altogether. But their patience and gentleness at close quarters impress him greatly. "There isn't a bite in them!"

Prince came from random parentage. He may also be getting a little deaf. To replace him with a thoroughbred pup could cost £50 or more. but at least there's less risk nowadays of having a good dog stolen. Paddy's father, Michael, once had a collie called Toss who was outstandingly good with cattle. On the eight miles of road to Louisburgh Fair, the dog would marshal the bullocks with unremitting discipline. Once arrived at the fair, he could be left in sole charge of them on the street while Michael went off for refreshment.

Such initiative and steadiness were widely remarked until one day, the dog disappeared. He came home two weeks later, from the direction of Killary, limping on bloodied front paws and trailing a halter of rope. He had, it seemed, torn his way out of captivity and swum the sea fiord from Connemara. The Connemara men have raided this coast down the years for everything from brides to potatoes and even today you wouldn't be up to them.

Toss does seem to have been rather special. When the road was being surfaced to the foot of the mountain and all the men were working at it, Toss would appear at the quarry at the time to knock off for dinner, to walk his master home. If Michael went visiting, the dog would seek out the house he was in and sit outside the door. And he had only to pick up the can at milking time for Toss to go running up the hill to bring the cows home from outside the mountain fence.

Less than twenty years ago, the ridge still had grazing for cattle. Paddy, who herded the cows there as a child, insists that fields and hill were "all the one green". But no one would dream of putting a cow on the mountain commonage now: it cannot carry even the sheep that are there.

It is easy to assume, without considering, that the mountains must have carried sheep for as long as the West has been farmed. But until the Scottish tenants arrived with their thousands of Blackface, sheep were kept only in small numbers and mainly for their wool. So the grazing of the hills is a comparatively modern land-use. But its thirteen decades have taken nutrition from the soil while giving nothing back. Now the sheep crowd shakily down in the spring, a quarter of their lambs are lost, and so little vegetation remains on the hills that the rain runs straight off in floods that rip the land to pieces.

Paddy is one of the few men on this side of the hill who feeds his ewes in winter. One reason for moving them round the ridge was to bring them to the troughs where he puts out beet pulp.

But the trouble with Blackface sheep is that they have to be taught to eat a concentrate. If you could get near enough to a mountain ewe to throw her a handful of pulp (which is a bit like All-Bran), she wouldn't even give it a sniff. To train his sheep to taste it, Paddy had to pen them for nights in a barn with nothing but pulp to eat and a pet lamb to show them it was edible. Even then there were ewes who turned up their noses and had to be kept in again.

Putting fifty ewes through boarding school is not, however, an exercise likely to impress the men who, each December, turn out flocks of six or seven hundred sheep to fend for themselves on the great tawny slopes of Mweelrea.

Strange Landmarks

NOTHING COULD SEEM more unchanging than the big sprawling strand below us, its permanence measured out in the flood and ebb of the tide. But between the convulsions of memorable storms, this long sweep of sand at the end of the boreen seems to shuffle its grains into new contours every day. If it is not being pounded and pawed by the sea, there is a flood in the channel from the mountain river, so that fresh and salt waves rush headlong at each other. And when the water stops churning and retreats, the wind gets to work, scouring the strand so fiercely that stones and shells are left perched atop little columns of sand, like a host of petrified mushrooms.

The strand has two strange landmarks, each surviving a mysterious past and both now succumbing, year by year, to the embrace of sand and sea.

The first, remarked by every visitor, is a conical mound about thirty feet high and crowned by a few feet of ancient masonry. It is all that remains of an old graveyard, made on a grassy promontory that the sea encircled and then began to whittle away. There are stories of skulls spilling out on the sand, and of coffins intercepted at sea by the fishermen of Inishturk.

Last year, Ethna and I stumbled up from the strand with a rough slab of slate which was used as a headstone by a journeyman mason in the year 1811. We thought it might be appreciated by the descendants of the family whose names were so handsomely carved on it. But there have been no takers for what could, I suppose, be regarded as a melancholy, if not actually ill-omened, keepsake.

In local lore, the graveyard was made at the site of an old monastery built by "renegade" monks from Inishbofin, the long, low island on our horizon. The story is qualified ironically in a footnote in Helen Waddell's "Medieval Latin Lyrics." It recalls that Colman, bishop of Lindisfarne (661-668), came back to Ireland and founded the monastery of Inishbofin with thirty Englishmen and many Irishmen who came back with him.

"But there was no peace among them, says Bede, for when the

summer and the time of harvest came the Irish took a desire of wandering, and then with the cold returned home to eat those things which their brethren had laboured in harvesting. And the contention was so strong that Colman built a new monastery for the English on the mainland, and no more is said of the improvident grasshoppers.'' It is the last of the Englishmen's homestead that we, having also withdrawn from the world to make our own harvests, now watch crumbling into the sea.

The second landmark on the strand fascinates us even more. Whenever we walk there at low tide, we find ourselves drawn to a jagged palisade that sticks up, stark and black, from the shelving sand. It is the wreck of an old wooden sailing vessel that we like to think belonged to the Armada. We keep a wave-worn piece of it, dried to silver, sitting on a book-case and once sent a chunk to the Ulster Museum in the vain hope that it could be dated.

The vessel came ashore opposite a line of reefs and islets that make these hazardous waters at the best of times. For most of the years we have known it, only a foot or two of its ribs has sketched its oval skeleton in the sand, the wood gnarled and black and hard as stone, fronded here and there with bladderwrack and frosted with white barnacles. Occasionally, as at the moment, the sand is swept away, exposing the forward ribs almost to the keel and showing them pierced for the wooden trenails that held the craft together. A neighbour who has measured the wreck when fully exposed to the stern puts its length at 87 feet — the size of a substantial inshore trawler.

The wreck has "always" been there, and almost the best reason for supposing it to date from the Armada is the lack of a better explanation. This is an area of vigorous and colourful oral tradition, as may be judged from Berry's "Tales Of The West", or Louisburgh's remarkable parish journal, *"An Choinneal*. The wreck of the River Dee, which came ashore with a cargo of timber in 1871, was promptly documented in a song and "there was many a telling on it." But beyond general belief that the lonely wreck below us was Spanish, and a neighbour's observation that the ballast was unusual and "like those stones from Greece in the pillars of Westport House", there is a singular lack of lore about it, which suggests that it predated the population driven west by Cromwell.

If it was an Armada vessel, it must have been one of the smallest — perhaps one of the 42 messenger boats that ran errands between the store ships and the big fighting galleons, such as El Gran Grin, wrecked off Clare Island and the Falcón Blanco of Inishbofin. Despite the intense Armada scholarship of recent years, there is still no full agreement on how many vessels actually ended up around Ireland's shores. There were at least 16 and possibly nine more.

Each time our wreck is uncovered to the keel, there is talk of an expedition by some of our neighbours — not to dig for bronze cannon or pewter plates but to amputate the choicest of the great oaken ribs. There are scars to show that this has happened in the past, but today the urgency seems to have gone out of it, so that before anyone actually reaches for a saw, the sand has closed in again.

What took us to the wreck this week was an outing with Báinin to visit the sea. In the weeks we have had him stabled, his life has been dull and sedentary. We had intended to leave him out on the hill, housing him only at night and in the worst of weather, so that at least he could have a gallop when he felt like it. But he hung about the hill so dolefully, gazing down at the house and getting wetter and wetter, that we brought him down and hinged a quarter of the stable door to give him a window on the world. Here he stands with head protruding, munching through a bale of hay every two or three days.

Báinin had grazed beside the strand in summer but had never actually set foot on it. He seemed torn between excitement and suspicion, at one moment kicking up his heels in play, at the next shying nervously from a clump of sea-rods or the sudden crash of a wave.

We debated setting him free of his bridle: with two miles of empty sand ahead of him and the spark of strand-racing in his blood, it seemed unfair not to let him off for a gallop on his own. But we decided against, afraid of trying to mix freedom and control in the one situation.

He found his own compensation. Pushing his nose into the sand and holding it there, he carved a furrow as he walked. Then, coming to a conclusion, he threw himself down at the end of his rein and took a long and sensuous sand-bath with all four hooves in the air.

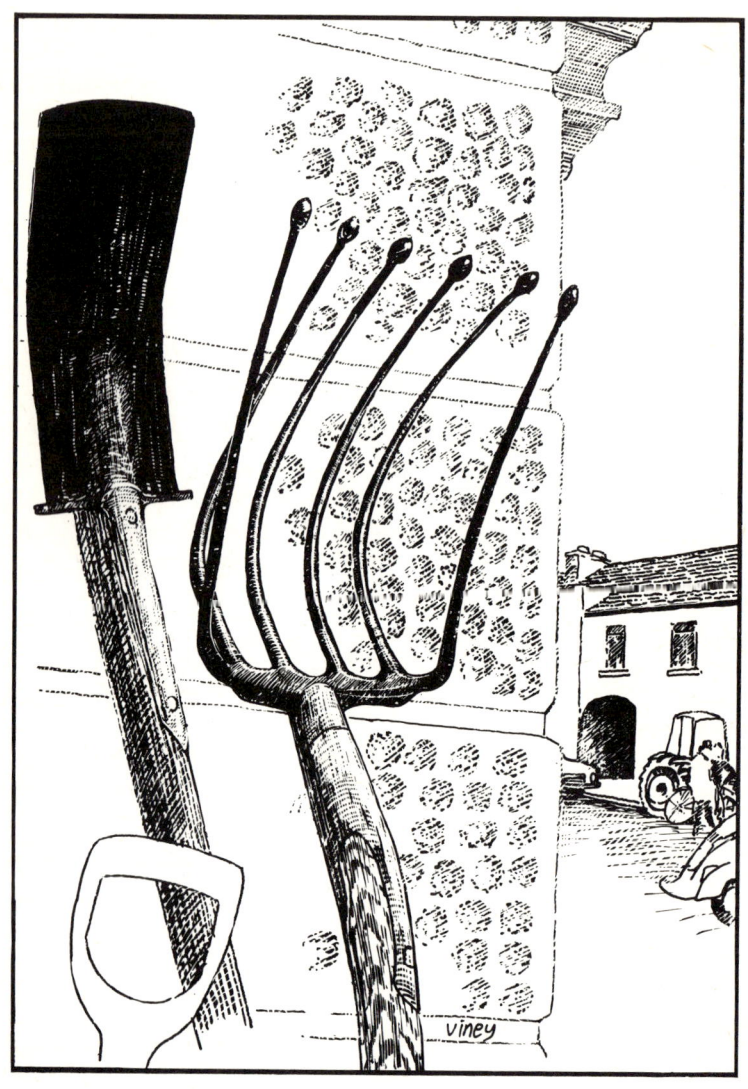

Trip to Town

WHEN THE CONVOY swung in beside us and the soldiers jumped down, it was the look on their faces that took me most aback: the young mouths set with tension, the young eyes burning bright, Their machine-guns wavered towards me as I advanced on the bank bearing two suspicious objects — the side handles of a scythe. For a moment I was quite bewildered: I have been so long away from it all. But Ethna goes into town more often: "It's only a cash delivery. You're out in the real world now."

We had managed to go a month without making a trip to Westport, the market town 22 miles up the coast. We keep a shopping list on the dresser and let it grow until some priority nags us into an expedition. This time it was early seed potatoes, which ought to be chitted for sowing next month.

Almost in self-parody, we smartened up for the day out. Unlike some of our neighbours, who travel to town for a haircut, we cut our hair to go to town. Even before we left Dublin, we had weaned ourselves from visits to the hairdressers. Ethna's skill with the scissors might not have sufficed in the era of the short-back-and-sides (though her mother, she remembers, used clippers on the neighbours in rural Cavan of the 1930s), but she keeps me kempt enough in these shaggier days, and her own hair, being curly, absorbs the occasional mistake. As a distraction, she splashed on one of the perfumes left over from the old life so that when she went to check Báinín's manger before we left, the pony sniffed uncertainly at a cloud of Dior-Dior.

The car at the gate is now so scabrous with rust that, on the rare occasions when we have to push it, we have to choose our hand-holds with some care. But it is, for the most part, mechanically indefatigable and pulls a load without fuss. We needed the trailer today to bring a quarter-ton of rolled barley (some for a neighbour) and a couple of bags of pony nuts. We normally buy our poultry feed from the little shop along at the bridge, but their supply has switched from barley to maize, which neither hens nor ducks seem to care for.

The road to Westport runs eight miles across moorland to Louisburgh and then winds along the coast of Clew Bay from Old

Head past the foot of Croagh Patrick. Each time I travel this way, another new bungalow seems to have appeared from nowhere, and eventually the ribbon of development will be virtually unbroken on the land side of the road. The landscape, like Ethna's curls, can fold in the occasional mistake: what would really spoil the character of this stretch of coast with its intimate hedgerows and infinite views, would be to widen and straighten the road.

There is one delight of these hedgerows that the summer tourist never sees — a variety of willow whose bare twigs gleam in winter in a vivid orange. It is a colour quite missing in our harsher landscape "out west", and as we rattled in through Lecanvey and Murrisk we stopped to pull a few glowing twigs to plant in a gulley on our acre. Nearly all willows grow very readily from cuttings and any piece of twig or branch, stuck upright in most soil, will take root and send out shoots.

After the seed potatoes and the animal feed bought at the farmers' co-op, we headed, as usual, for the hardware emporium on the hill. A four-pound bag of nails is a routine replenishment, but this time I was buying three prime implements of our new way of life: the spade, the scythe and the turf fork.

We came to Mayo with two garden spades bought in Dublin. One had a long handle and a straight blade and another a short handle and a blade so wide it was almost square. The latter was called a "Bulldog" and must have been designed for short, square Britons: but Ethna adopted it happily. The other spade at least suited my size and I saw nothing wrong with it — until I met the *loy*.

This is no more than a spade in Irish and standard usage hereabouts: it is the local *loy* itself which is so special. It is Messrs Darby's "Leenane" spade, as distinct from their "Achill" or "Sligo" — all names which denote regional differences in design. The narrow blade of the "Leenane" is both curved and slightly hollowed and widens a little towards the tip. When burnished with use, it can shine like a silver spoon.

But its shape has practical virtues. One of the chief uses for a spade in these parts is on the bog, where it is needed for scrawing — cutting away the top spit to expose the peat — and levelling up the successive steps in cutting. My straight spade makes all of this much harder work than it needs to be. I have to stoop lower when scrawing and the spade gives me no leverage in ripping the top sod free. And when I am chopping out wet peat, to prepare a level surface for the sléan, my spade refuses to let go of it — whereas the curve of the *loy* breaks the vacuum and lets the lump fly free.

There are more advantages to the *loy* even in ordinary gardening — I can see it replacing the hoe, for example, when I am skinning the land of weeds — but it was last year's hard slog on the mountain that made me resolve to buy one. The turf fork, with its thimble-capped tines, is another tool that saves time and labour. I have always thought it an exceptionally handsome implement and anything that can shift half-a-dozen sods at one throw is worth investing in. We have gone on long enough borrowing tools from our neighbours.

Looking for a scythe in February, with the grass only stirring into growth, seemed to make me something of an oddity. Looking for a scythe with the old-fashioned wooden handle, rather than the standard modern one of tubular steel, merely confirmed it. But ever since I swung the scythe belonging to my neighbour, Joe, a man even taller than I and twice as wide, nothing would do me but the length and balance of a wooden shaft.

Neither of the town's big hardware stores could help me, nor even the farmers' co-op. But I found a handle at last in a corner store lined with pints of stout. It cost me a modest £1.40 — but the blade, from Austria, was over £5.00. And to find the *dúirnins* — the two side handles fitted to the shaft with metal rings — I had to travel to yet another hardware shop to buy what were reputedly the very last *dúirnins* in Westport, at £1.50 each.

It was these tokens of pastoral Ireland that I carried into confrontation with the lethal urban hardware of the 1980s.

Scents of Spring

SO THIS IS how the spring should be! The fuchsia already breaking into leaf, ahead even of the thorn-bush. And the flush of green creeps up the hills so that even the high, lean fields are striped with young grass where the ripples of the old lazy-beds give shelter. A breeze from the mountain brings the cloying tobacco-scent of silage, and I see Jack, the donkey, moving in an aureole of sun as he hauls the blue cart of fodder up the boreen. This year, there should be no hungry gap between fermented grass and fresh.

Silage, sheep-dip and tractor-smoke are the three scents of man on this hillside. But the smell that will recall this spring to me is new and far sweeter. I have been building things with wood so fresh from the pine forests that it coats my hands with resin and surrounds me with a fragrance — of Christmas bath-cubes — forgotten since childhood.

Forestry slabs, the outer slices of spruce trunks sold off as waste by the saw-mills, come in great bales tied with neat metal ribbons. Even as firewood they are good value. But I have been using them for all kinds of construction, like a smallholder's Lego. I began with the pony's stable, where the slabs built a sturdy partition and a manger. Then I bridged the stream where the flood had torn the banks away, splicing the heaviest slabs into a 10-foot span. Next, I remade the compost bins, improvised until now from concrete blocks or sheep wire.

The latest and grandest construction is The Fence — a palisade that staggers alongs the seaward ditch of our acre, raising its shelter to a height of six feet. The fence is not solid — that would be disastrous — but leaves gaps the same width as the slabs for the wind to whistle through. A reader who has used this kind of paling in his mountain garden in Connemara promises that it will cut the wind's velocity by half even 65 feet from the fence.

At that kind of performance, I was not too concerned with appearances: if the homestead began to look like the OK Corral, so be it. But everywhere the slabs have been used, they look right. They remind us, at the same time, how rare are the trees in this rocky landscape and how little wood has been available for rough construction. My fence has become an advertisement for what is virtually a new material, and our neighbours, thinking of sheep-folds and barn walls, have shown more than polite interest in it.

March is the month when the hares go courting and gather, sometimes six or seven together, to play ring-a-ring-a-roses in the middle of open meadows. Last year, we could watch their romping from the doorstep. But, so far this spring, the hares have been unaccountably scarce. Instead and on the same ground across the hedge, we have been watching the strange, sinuous ballet of two black cats.

They are toms from the neighbouring farms, vying for the favour of our own cat, Sooty. When not leaping and twining in their rapt *pas-de-deux*, they hold menacing poses for impossible lengths of time, crooning *mantras* of intimidation, while Sooty sits demurely apart to await the outcome.

She is also a black-and-white cat, misleadingly small and dainty. She is actually a practised killer, kept efficient by need: we feed her little and put her out at night to hunt. We have found her chewing rats and jackdaws, but her most impressive prey to date was a rabbit as big as herself. She hid the body under a tarpaulin and, days later, arrived on the doorstep with the skin, from which both meat and bones had been deftly extracted.

We tend to take sides between her suitors, since one of them has kept her company faithfully through the winter and it seems unfair that he should now have to beat off a rival. But at least they will have some chance to mate with her, which would not have been the case a year ago. Sooty's lover last spring — and father, indeed, of several generations of cats on most of the farms this side of the hill — was a great, grey, feral cat that no ordinary tom dare go near.

Ireland does not have the true European wildcat, *Felis silvestris*, though one keeper of the National Museum, Robert Scharff, never lost his hope that it might turn up in the mountain fastnesses of Connacht. The wildcat does survive, even without protection, in the grouse-moor and sheep-farming country of Scotland's lower hills, where it is probably more abundant than at any time in living memory.

Felis silvestris is about a third larger than a domestic cat and has a bushy, blunt-ended tail with thick bands of black. But when the domestic cat goes feral, or wild — sleeping rough, so to speak, and living off the land — he is also likely to be among the biggest of his kind; indeed, I have read that he may actually grow in weight and power. The feral tom I met among the cabbages last spring was certainly the biggest cat I have ever seen, and the most intimidating, with a great square head and unfriendly amber eyes

At the time he came to court Sooty — to mesmerize her, as it looked to us — we had no idea of his criminal antecedents. Only when we found one of our ducks with her head torn off did neighbours relate their own losses in preceding months: a dozen chickens in a night had not been too many for the ghostly grey outlaw. They urged me, should he come to call again, to blast him apart with my shotgun. But soon afterwards he was cornered in a barn along the road and came exactly to that end.

As Sooty grew heavy with kittens, we became concerned for her. Our last cat had died while giving birth to stillborn kittens, and now we had exposed her diminutive successor to the attentions of a monster. But she bore the kittens without fuss, and by the time they were weaned they were almost as big as her. Of their father's wild nature there was no sign, and the one who went to the city has done rather well for himself — as a mouser in a fashionable foodstore.

Far-Off Voices

How do you measure remoteness? Ten years ago, I would have said said that the remotest place I knew was the empty island of Inishvickillane, at the far edge of the Blaskets, where I once camped alone for a few weeks among the seals and sea-pinks. Since then, Charles Haughey has built a holiday home there, and sometimes uses a helicopter to land him at the door. I wish him well of the island, and long may his red deer rut among the bracken — but Inishvickillane can never be as remote for him as once it was for me.

Remoteness worries some people. They ask us concerned questions about doctors, hospitals and schools. Even some of Thoreau's visitors, coming to his cabin in the woods, used to brood on what could happen if he fell sick or cut himself. "To them, life seemed full of danger," he wrote, "and you would suppose that they would not go a-huckleberrying without a medicine chest." Our nearest doctor is eight miles away, but the car and the telephone — like the helicopter and the school bus — have made remoteness relative. Only as transport and communication become costly does distance regain its old significance.

Our corner of *Iar Umhal* does have a special aura of remoteness — "as if civilisation has fled", thought an ecstatic travel writer in a recent *Sunday Times*. It is not just the four-and-a-half hours of the drive from Dublin or the steady attenuation of the road once it has passed John Healy's Charlestown in mid-Mayo.

It is more that the destination seems constantly withheld. The first buffet of Atlantic wind may be felt around Bohola, but even after reaching the coast at Westport there is another 10 miles, and then another, until that theatrical bend at the top of the hill that sends the eye soaring over an oddly primeval composition of mountains, sand and sea. Remoteness needs some thrill of arrival.

That same bend, as it happens, marks out another kind of remoteness. It is the limit, more or less, of the line-of-sight reception of the new RTE 2 television signal beamed out from the mountains of Achill. The signal now brings the second channel into most of the homes of west Mayo, but leaves the community on this side of the hill still untouched by "Coronation Street".

Well, perhaps not entirely. The mountains that shut us out from the world abound in fragmented television signals fluttering like moths along the dark walls. At Leenane on the Killary, for example, just one house on the edge of the village can get a viewable picture of any sort, while its neighbours can pick up nothing. So while RTE 1 reaches our rooftop straight and clear from Clifden, a snowy simulacrum of RTE 2 bounces off the shoulder of Mweelrea from Gort and can be caught, unexpectedly, on the prongs of a rabbit's-ears aerial.

Sometimes we are made to feel that, having abjured the city and its ways, we should not "bother" with television at all, but should, instead, spend our evenings at rushwork, candle-dipping, macramé and other crafts so typical of rural Irish life. This might, at times, head off our keener frustrations with the medium, but it would also close our young daughter's window on the world.

I sometimes wonder how this would affect her imagination and its matching of pictures to facts. My childhood was spent in a city and its cinemas; television, when it came, extended an already rich experience. It is hard to imagine the cognitive world of our grandparents, especially those in remote rural districts, in which the mind strove to animate the illustrations on a printed page. It would surely be perverse to want to send our daughter back to that. For all our impatience with "Popeye" or "Charlie's Angels'," there comes the moment when, at the end of "The Voyage of the Beagle," she asks to read a book called "On The Origin Of Species".

We ourselves would sacrifice television more readily than radio, the medium that most informs us and that keeps us nourished with the music we like. Radio may not depend on line-of-sight reception, but it is difficult enough to tune in distant stations from below a mountain barrier. It is here that the external wire aerial, virtually unknown to an urban generation nurtured on VHF transistors, comes back into its own.

We have a good battery transistor, which I often take with me when I am working out of doors. In the days when I caught the Number 25 home and sat on the top deck seething at the barrage from the factory girls' transistors (well, of *course* they were factory girls, my dear — one had only to *listen!*), the idea of taking the radio out of doors in my beloved Connacht would have seemed a vulgar heresy. But now that I spend so much time labouring alone, Gay Byrne is often hung on the hedge while I am digging, or Rodney Rice propped on a tussock while I am at the turf.

But amiable company as Gay, Rodney and Liam may be, they do not satisfy our deeper needs for information and analysis of what is happening in the world and for generous doses of classical music. For all its enterprising use of the international telephones, the RTE newsroom cannot begin to compete with the depth and authority of the BBC World Service, broadcasting on short wave.

And, as for music, we find RTE radio thoroughly cowed by an operatic Mafia with a taste for virgin sopranos and prone, when compiling programmes for "popular" ears, to reach yet again for "Your Hundred Best Orchestral Tunes". Our taste is not especially highbrow and certainly not modern, but for a balanced intake of instrumental music we could not do without the BBC Third Programme.

For either the World Service or the Third, we have to stay within earshot of the kitchen and a radio that, while less than 20 years old, must already qualify as an antique. The Schaub-Lorenz was one of the last and best of the big table sets using valves, and if it lives on the kitchen dresser as long as its forebears of the Thirties and Forties, we shall be well pleased.

The secret of our reception, however, which must be considered miraculous by most west-coast standards, is a contraption presented to us for Christmas by our friend Gustin, the Leonardo of Inishbofin. It is a revolving web of aerial wire about a yard across and with a tuner in the middle — the sort of thing that would have got you shot as a spy in the last war. Plugged into our Schaub-Lorenz, it brings us not only the BBC, but the whole spectrum of cold-war propaganda, from Voice of America to Radio Tirana. No remote, self-sufficient home should be without one.

Running Low

AT THE END of yet another cloudless day (the sea aglow with turquoise, the islands lost in haze), the pony moved restlessly around the water hole at the bottom of his field. We were watching him idly from the kitchen window, remarking that his coat is getting almost as white as the rocks about him on the hillside, when the question suddenly occurred: did the hole have any water? I set off up the road with a full bucket and Báinin came to meet me. I was scarcely through the gate before his nose was in the bucket: he emptied half of it without lifting his head.

When a pony gets thirsty on the moister slopes of Mayo, it is time for people to look to their water supply. At the little waterfall below the bridge, our stream is now reduced to a single, splashing thread. Our neighbours assure us that it never dries, even in the longest drought, being fed by a spring from the cavernous heart of the hill. So long as it keeps topping up the high pools there will be water in the pipe and enough to feed the sprinkler. But other streams along the ridge have a less certain reputation and one has to peer closely between the rocks to see any movement at all.

At one such stream last week, I worked with a friend for a couple of days to build a water tank, a substantial cistern to store the slightest trickle. We chose a natural hollow beside the bed of the stream and dug out a hole about seven feet by nine. Those rocks we could not lift we moved by using a beam as a lever, grateful that they would budge at all. When the hole was three feet deep, we gave it a floor of cement, partly for fear that the blue clay would come "boiling up" again, as it has a habit of doing in this locality.

I am still appalled by the sheer quantity of materials that go into any piece of building — the more so when they have to be moved about by hand. To build the tank took 150 concrete blocks, seven hundredweight bags of cement and countless bags of sand. These were hauled up the first meadow by tractor and thrown or hoisted over a stone wall. From there the hillside became a good deal steeper and rougher and my Ballbarrow came into play, proving once again that it is a great deal more than a pretty plastic toy. At the end of a hundred trips up the hill I was weary enough, but to have attempted it with a conventional steel barrow would have reduced me to collapse.

When the tank was completed and plastered inside, its capacity was 84 cubic feet — enough, if I have got my cubic centimetres right, to hold something over 500 gallons. We built a dam and a sluice and fixed a grille to keep stones from filling the tank when the floods come back again. It was hard to imagine that the stream could ever come back to its old, torrential self; when we turned its feeble murmur into the tank, it took a whole day to fill it.

From our perch on the sunny hillside, we looked out across a sea of high pressure and easterly offshore winds. The first salmon boat from Connemara had taken up its mark between the islands and our talk turned to fishing and swimming — or rather, why so notoriously few of the Irish who live beside the Atlantic ever learn to swim.

Professor John C. Messenger, the American anthropologist who studied the lives and *mores* of the people of Inisheer in the Aran Islands in the early 1960s, could not find a single islander who could swim. The currach fishermen offered "folk rationalisations" in explanation: "Better for a man to drown at once and save himself the suffering", or "The man who can't swim will take more care." (I could add to these, from my sojourn across the bay in Connemara at about the same time, the tradition that "The sea must have its own", too literal an interpretation of which had left men to drown within sight of their neighbours.)

The most significant reason why the men of Inisheer couldn't swim was, insisted Messenger, never broached. It was "the puritancial reluctance to bare the body either publicly or privately at any age."

Here in Mayo, it is true, there is no great readiness to whip off shirt and vest the moment the weather is right. I may do so occasionally myself, in the early summer before the flies start biting, but not without feeling somewhat out of step with my neighbours. The sun tan is, after all, an aesthetic of urban deprivation — which may explain why, when the Mayo lads cross to Britain, their bronzing torsos decorate the trenches in the city excavations.

But the reasons why they grow up unable to swim seem quite straightforward. First, the small-farm childhood — even beside the sea — is far too busy and filled with chores. It has been a sad revelation to our young daughter to find that the children here, once home on the school bus, are not sent off to play. They have work to do in the house or around the farm.

Second, the strands are not seen as a playground. I have never once met children on the shore unless they lived beside it and were gathering sea-rods for pocket-money. My companion on the hill had been such a child, gathering periwinkles to sell or fishing from the rocks — but never learning to swim.

My own childhood, in the English resort of Brighton, was spent beside a safer and more amiable sea. My playtime was my own, the beaches were crowded with bathers and I learned to swim by trying, day after day. But here along this rugged, empty shore, even the Sunday outings to the Silver Strand have only a ritual walk in the mind; never a swim. There is no one to teach or even to set example.

The drought nearly cost us our turf this week. Like most families, we still have much of last year's turf in footings and stacks on the bog and are trying to clear it to make room for new cuttings. It is dried at last by the spring wind and sun. A few days ago, returning home from the other side of the hill, we were appalled to see a great cloud of smoke billowing up from the mountain.

Binoculars showed me a bright orange line of fire advancing downhill from the ridge, fanned onwards by a stiff north-easterly breeze. There were men silhouetted in the smoke, beating at the flames. I found a shovel and we drove off to the bog road. But by the time I reached the top, the fire had been flailed to a halt. The track of it spread in a huge black stain a mile across — and the edge of it had come within 200 yards of our hard-won turf.

The Hungry Gap

THE LAST OF the courgettes came out of the freezer this week, just as the courgette seedlings on the window-sill were making their second true leaves, ready for planting out. The conjunction was satisfying — not because we specially want to eat courgettes all the year round, but because I seem to be getting the cycle of sufficiency somewhere near right at last.

This is the testing time, the "hungry gap" of early summer, when the stores of last year's vegetables are coming to an end and the voice from the kitchen is wondering again when we shall be getting something from the garden. Not for us, in our voluntary frugality, the Italian carrots at 30p a pound, or the Cypriot new potatoes at 15p, to say nothing of £2 for petrol for the round trip to town.

There is nothing much wrong in any case with our own old potatoes — either the tasty, floury Records or the red-skinned Desiree (these grown for their reputation of keeping well at the end of the year). Both are as firm as the day they were harvested. Some were left out on the ridges too long, so that we must give the green bits to the hens and use the rest to make boxty.

Boxty, indeed, is such an excellent way of using old chunks of potatoes — with which most city cooks are also faced at this time of year — that our way of making these delicious pancakes may be of interest. If we had to make it in the traditional manner, by grating the potatoes laboriously, we would not have it very often. But one piece of equipment brought with us from the old life is the Kenwood kitchen mixer, which can liquidise four pounds of potatoes in a few seconds. Then we stir in a fistful of flour and a good pinch of salt, and melt a fragment of margarine in the frying pan.

Boxty cooked over electricity seems not nearly so good as boxty cooked on a solid-fuel range. This is more than mere sentiment: there is something in the quality of the range's heat that toasts the boxty to golden perfection. However, you cook them, turn when you see the potato darkening from beneath and serve hot with plenty of butter. One or two cakes of boxty will satisfy most people, but I often eat four or five — a gluttony excused by a more robust lifestyle.

As the freezer yields us its last bags of leeks, of French and runner beans, and a final, overlooked, pack of peas, what else have we to eat?

There is still a tea-chest full of celeriac, the knobbly, turnip-sized roots that taste like the heart of celery and get sweeter the longer they lie in the sand. And under a thatch of rushes is a mound of Swede turnips, seemingly indestructible since I discovered how to treat the boron deficiency that used to rot them away.

But what can actually be picked in the garden is not now very much. We left the Brussels sprouts to shoot again, and these delicious sprigs enlivened our meals for weeks. The sprouting broccoli played their part, too, but would have done better with more shelter through the winter: the winds had almost twisted them out of the ground. The kale and winter cauliflower could have done with more dung. And the spring cabbage that should be hearting now was wiped out altogether this winter: a salt gale withered a hundred seedlings in a night.

So the green plant that succours us through the hungry gap is the resilient Swiss chard, otherwise called seakale beet or silver beet. It is a "rootless" beetroot, eaten for its crinkly, succulent leaves with their wide and juicy midribs. It is rarely seen in shops, certainly in this country, because it is such a bulky crop and wilts within 24 hours. Until we first grew it ourselves, last spring, we had never tasted it; now, it is as much a staple crop as cabbage.

Chard is sometimes described as an easier "substitute" for spinach, as if it were in some way inferior. But even apart from its taste and texture, which we think is better, chard has more iron than spinach, broccoli or kale, three times as much riboflavin as cabbage and five times as much Vitamin C as lettuce. It is also one of the first crops to burst into life in spring. The chard we have been eating since March was sown last August and will carry through to July, when the spring-sown crop takes over.

Among the crops laid down in the freezer last autumn were some twenty pounds of blackberries, picked from the ditches of our acre. They were meant mainly for fruit juice, rich in Vitamin C, which our daughter could take to school. But even under the guise of ribena, it proved an eccentricity intolerable to her fellow eleven-year-olds. Goat's milk has been a little better, though greeted generally with horror and disgust, but we refuse to bow to the rural orthodoxy of sugary orange squash.

There was no doubt in our minds, meanwhile, what should be done with the redundant blackberries. Once we had tasted the blackberry wine we made at harvest-time, it was a quick step to wondering if frozen blackberries would serve as well.

Made with the minimum of sugar (just two-and-a-half pounds to the gallon) and fermented with a Bordeaux wine yeast, our blackberry wine is, we think, to be compared with any *vin rose* — mellow, slightly sparkling, with a delightful aftertaste of the fruit itself. It also, needless to say, spreads a fine warmth through the stomach.

It followed the heady success of our elder-flower wine, a fragrant distillation of summer. We shall be out to the hedgerows again next month to gather bucketfuls of creamy blossom.

Encouraged by the product of frozen blackberries, we turned next to the packets at the very bottom of the freezer. They held pallid chunks of Florence fennel, a crop I grew last spring without much success. The bulbs of the fennel can be a sweet and tender vegetable with the aniseedy flavour of the herb. But mine grew rankly in a wet summer and went woody.

On the principle that wine can be made — or, at least, alcohol produced — from almost anything that grows, we put the Florence fennel through the recipe used for celery wine. On sampling so far, it may take some considerable time — if ever — to turn into Pernod.

Feeling Good

BEFORE THE SUN rises from the ridge over Six Noggins, it reaches through the gaps in the mountains to light up the islands, one by one. Then the very rim of the shore takes fire and the long strand below us slowly incandesces from purple to hot pink to creamy gold. Admiring all this from the carrot patch the other morning, where I was weeding and contemplating by turns, the impulse suddenly took hold: I would go for a dip before breakfast.

To convey the full, noble romanticism of this idea. it must be said that the number of times I have actually swum in the seas around Ireland could be counted on ten numb fingers. As a youth, I was almost a daily communicant with the English Channel, but later I became corrupted by holidays spent snorkelling off Greece and Spain. I tried the mask and flippers once off Connemara, lured by the crystal clarity of sea, and found myself diving down through water so cold that it burned the nerves.

Tucked away, nonetheless, in the propectus of our new life was an image of myself as an early-morning swimmer. In Dublin, it would not have occurred to me to join the hearty walruses at the Forty Foot; that kind of togetherness did not attract. At the Atlantic, however, where a man could swim as solitary as a seal, my youthful affair with the sea might be revived.

Our first two years did not encourage it. Fine summer days came rarely and one at a time; there was no spell of warmth to let the impulse germinate. But now, at six-thirty on a quiet May morning, the will was there, if inclined to flicker somewhat in the cool breeze from the mountain. Rather than risk irresolution by walking to the strand, I took the bicycle from the shed and rattled off down the stony boreen, startling the cattle and sending the spring lambs running through the fields.

The sun at this moment cleared the ridge like an arc-lamp and my shadow leaped ahead between the blackthorn blossom and the yellow flags. At the farm beside the strand, the breeze was soughing in the sycamores. I braked, reconsidering, then rattled on again.

I have written before about the awesome scale of the strand. It stretches wings of sand from a great central delta, so that one's footprints, from the boreen to the water's edge, stretch for three or four hundred paces. It is not a place for those who, in restaurants, must have a chair with its back to the wall, or who when venturing to bathe seek out the little cove, the cranny in the rocks. To go swimming here is to brave an arena.

At that hour, in that intimate golden light, with the silent hills behind me, the edge of the sea was the most private place in the world. Even so, it felt strange to strip off in the middle of all that space — like undressing on the stage of a deserted amphitheatre.

For once there was no swell and thus no breakers: just the regular lift and froth of quiet waves. It was not an occasion for a wild whoop and a charge, nor for loitering and wincing, but for steady, stoical advance. There is a branch of yoga which insists that the seat of man's strength and spirit lies just above his stomach, and wading into the Atlantic in May before breakfast is a good way of proving it. When, after no great time, I emerged from the water and jogged around to dry, the breeze from the mountain was positively warm.

I felt very good; exhilarated beyond all expectation. Indeed, at the risk of sounding even more like a middle-aged Narcissus, this Spring has brought me an unprecedented sense of physical well-being. The swim was, in one way, a celebration of it. It seems that manual labour can bring one to the point of actual pleasure in exertion and a buoyancy even in repose.

Athletes must know this feeling very well, and can set out to maintain it even in city life. I think of Noel Carroll, radiating fitness to his generally sedentary fellow men in Dublin, and recognise that the kind of well-being he has earned on the running track is what has come to me by way of *loy* and shovel.

It has taken almost three years of living — as it seemed to one recent visitor — "like an over-enthusiastic Mezzogiorno peasant" — to remake in this dramatic fashion a 45-year-old body, poorly maintained, undermined by decades of booze and heavy smoking and never very stalwart to begin with. As a teenager, I took up Charles Atlas on his promise that I, too, could have a body like his. But his mail-order exercises began to take so much time that I ended up with a presentable set of shoulders and not much else. Only now, for example, are there muscles around my stomach, so that I can boast of a 34-inch waist that even a tailor would have to believe.

Recent recruits to this chronicle may be wondering why I should have been out weeding the carrots at six-thirty in the morning. In fact, I had begun at five, when sunrise was no more than a glow in the sky beyond Mweelrea.

It is now six months since we decided, along with Tom Moore, that
> *The best of all ways*
> *To lengthen our days*
> *Is to steal a few hours from the night,*
> *my dear.*

We adapted to this with remarkable ease, both having the kind of metabolism that makes for morning alertness. Indeed, it now seems so natural that we have to make an effort to understand why anyone should find it strange. Of all the great changes we have made in our lives, none seems to disconcert — even, in some odd way, alarm — other people quite so much as our having reorganised time to suit ourselves.

It was inevitable, as the mornings grew brighter and more alluring, and the fieldwork built up to its seasonal peak, that I should be drawn out into the dew to start gardening. The difficulty is to stop at the other end of the day. Thoreau used to be out at five to start hoeing his beans — but he made sure to stop at noon, to sit in the sun and think. I am likely to be there at sunset, still happily raking away.

Little Luxuries

A FEW WEEKS AGO a friend who lives, somewhat graciously, on a few stately acres in Kildare went looking for the bed of asparagus she had encouraged her gardener to plant last year. She found the bed, but no asparagus. The gardener was only moderately apologetic. When he was a boy, he said, he had learned his trade at another big house with asparagus. "And the old lady, she used to stand over me while I weeded it, poking me with her stick to show me the bits I'd missed."

Coming to the asparagus bed this spring and hunting for the tiny spears to see where it was safe to weed, this rancorous memory had floated over him. "And I dug 'em up again!" he declared, with a look that quelled all comment, and he retreated stiffly to the greenhouse.

Arriving now at my ridges of two-year-old asparagus, and trying to sort its ferns from a rug of invading grass, I have to be glad that I did not, after all, persevere with trying to grow half an acre of it.

When we were planning our rural economy, it had seemed the ideal cash crop: a luxury vegetable with a high profit margin for the smallholder who didn't cost his own time. In 1978, when I sowed the first of it, a half-acre would have returned £250. The plants would take four years to mature to the first crop, but then would go on yielding every spring for 15 years or more. There were only 20 acres of asparagus in the whole Republic, and I could use the time while the plants developed to find a market among the posher country hotels.

In a giant seed-bed, finely raked, I sowed the first instalment of the 5,000 plants it would take to fill half an acre — some 2,000 seeds dropped individually, one every two inches, on my hands and knees. Half of the plants would have to be scrapped later on, since only the male asparagus is held to be worth keeping. When the seedlings appeared — fragile spears no bigger than a bodkin — the two of us spent days on our knees to weed them.

Last spring we were kneeling again, wrenching up weeds from rows that should have been bristling with ranks of elfin weaponry but which, unaccountably, were not. It had been a savage winter, but Connacht escaped the worst of it — and asparagus, as a maritime plant, is meant to flourish in salty ocean winds. Perhaps, at this infant stage, the autumn gales had been too severe. At all events, of a couple of thousand seedlings, scarcely more than a hundred survived to be planted on.

It was just as well. As my estimates of what I had to plant to feed us for a year became more realistic, and the hens and ducks began to insist on adequate *lebensraum,* it grew obvious that we did not have half an acre to spare. There is room in the rotation for a rood of barley, but otherwise our field is full.

It had also become obvious that no one who does not want to spend half his life on his knees should set out to establish asparagus in newly-turned pasture — not, that is, if he is an organic gardener who wants to do without chemicals.

I could have made all my cultivation a great deal easier by dousing the whole field at the outset, from ditch to ditch, with a total weedkiller (perhaps, if one could get it in Ireland, with ammonium sulphamate, potent against docks and couch grass and decaying in the ground into sulphate of ammonia.) But I preferred to have the land ploughed and sown with potatoes and to extirpate the perennial weeds as the years went by. It is not a way that suits perennial plantations of crops such as asparagus and strawberries.

On the farm below us, next to the strand, there is a meadow sheltered by sycamores, where each July I join a *meitheal* for silage-making. In this meadow, 40 years ago, flourished half an acre of strawberries — a cash crop carried 20 miles to market in a side-car. It was a remarkable crop to be grown on this remote farm at such a time, but it was worth all of £50. It was grown without sprays and weeded by hand, often for 12 hours a day. The farmer wore trousers with padded knees, of a kind I have been meaning to make myself.

Strawberries do especially well here, since the ocean winds are free of viruses, and our own small plot of them, wreathed in white blossom for weeks, is now weighted down with fruit. It was a visitor of the "no-digging" school, privileged herself to have a walled garden and an ample supply of spoiled hay for deep mulching, who urged me last autumn to lay down old newspapers between the rows of strawberry plants as a mulch against winter weeds. I put down a liberal thickness of the *Sunday Times* and scattered it with heavy stones. By Christmas, the hedges were festooned with shredded newsprint and the scree of stones lay on to be gathered in the spring.

To weed strawberries is to confirm one's suspicion that weeds tend to hide among the crops they most resemble. Intertwined at the heart of the plants are giant specimens of creeping buttercup, their leaves, at a glance, indistinguishable, and the bare disks of daisies masquerade among the unripe berries.

One by one, the common perennial weeds are giving up their hold, and I am left to fight irruptions of wild plants one would never normally think of as weeds. This summer, whole days have been given to clearing marsh woundwort, a herb which throws up stout stems two or three feet high and has leaves once recommended as a healing poultice for scythe-cuts. It infiltrates my finely-tilled ridges with creeping, fleshy rootstocks like white, arthritic snakes. Touch one and it snaps, each piece to start a new Medusa.

Sifting out such horrors is a chore. But there are times when weeding is sheer therapy: on summer days after rain, when the earth slides through the fingers like cool velvet, when the purple dead-nettles are droning with companionable bumble-bees, and the raw geometry of the vegetable beds is found, after all, to hold survivors of the old, wild meadow — iridescent vetch and fragile fumitory, pink geranium and red clover, a cushion of forget-me-nots in a haze of sapphire stars.

Thelwell Days

IF THELWELL HAD found himself at the Louisburgh Horse Show the other Sunday, his cartoonist's instinct might have drawn him to the judging of Class 27: Best Pony, 12.2h.h. or under, shown in hand by children under 13 years of age; 1st prize £10. There he could have spotted an affecting incongruity: in a row of dainty equine miniatures, with ribboned manes and braided tails, loomed a burly Connemara gelding with his mane blowing the wrong way, looking as out of place as a navvy at a garden party. The small girl struggling to hold him in line wore distinctly baggy jodhpurs (for growing into) and her red hair escaped from a riding hat that gave similar room for expansion. Her expression as she awaited the judges displayed, I liked to think, the true grit of the classic Thelwell heroine.

It had needed considerable grit, indeed, for her to be there in the line at all. When she mooted the idea of entering the show a couple of months ago, we gave her no encouragement. We disapproved, we said stuffily, of competing in things one has, rather than in things one does (especially, we added silently, when there isn't a hope of winning). Besides, we didn't think Báinin was ready for a horse show. It was this pushed her shoulders back. He *would* be ready — we'd see!

The pony's schooling, with our daughter in the saddle, had recently been taken in hand by a neighbour, an experienced horsewoman, who lives a mile along the road towards the mountain. If only we would let her ride over, Michele pleaded, she and Báinin would get a lot more lessons. Eventually, with more casualness than we felt, we let her go, riding for the first time unaccompanied. Between us and this neighbour is the one really worrying bit of the road, where it narrows between dry-stone walls and has almost no verges. What if she met the bread-van in a hurry, or that young fellow in the scarlet Mini? We watched her go, a tiny figure in the sprawling landscape, and checked her past each ESB pole until she dwindled out of sight. "Listen all the time!" we told her.

In the next few weeks she met them all: the tractors and trailers shuttling to and from the bog, the fish van, the secondary school bus, the huge lorry coming for sea-rods, the tourist with a caravan. At first, when she heard a distant engine over the sounds of wind and sea, she would slide down out of the saddle and pull the pony in to the side. But surprisingly soon, as Báinin got used to different shapes, colours and reverberations, she could stay in the saddle, waving drivers to slow as I had instructed her. Not all of them paid atention. "There was this *woman!* She had a GB on her car and she went *whooshing* by at fifty miles an hour!" For all her apparent poise in the saddle, she would sometimes come home with a headache or in oddly imperious mood: an eleven-year-old, too, can know tension.

But given such determination, and her very real progress, we had to agree to the Horse Show and let preparations begin. There were "slippers" to be fitted to Báinin's front feet — the thin, old shoes used in these parts as a pony's introduction to shoeing. The local part-time blacksmith carried out the job at our front gate (the days of "hot" shoeing at the forge have vanished from this locality). Báinin submitted well to all the paring and hammering, we had lifted and handled his feet in readiness for just this day.

His spring moult had cast off the hair matted and stained from the winter's stabling and left him in his third year a paler shade of grey. His coat had even lost the moth-holes worn by his nibbling at last year's ticks. But it still needed plenty of grooming with curry comb and dandy brush to get rid of all the tangles. On the day before the show his tail and mane were shampooed and his forelock — to my dismay — trimmed back out of his eyes. But I drew the line at plaiting and ribboning, and as he set out on the eight miles to Louisburgh, ridden by our neighbour's teenage daughter, he was more or less as God made him.

Louisburgh Horse Show grows more stylish every year, bringing horses in boxes from all over Connacht. We had no notion of competing with the "quality", but had tried to enter Báinin among the local "agricultural" ponies, which was where, as we saw it, he belonged. But his breed disqualified him — an insult, I should have thought, to the tradition of working Connemaras — and, there being no Connemara category that suited, Báinin ended up among the posh children's ponies. What most discomfited Michele was not that she lacked a proper riding jacket, white gloves and hairnet, but that she couldn't show Báinin from the saddle.

At least she does appreciate how lucky she is to have such a pony in such a place as this. If we have been living out some of the dreams of a good many desk-bound Dubliners, she can play the heroine, not merely of a Thelwell cartoon but of an Eilis Dillon adventure story. Each morning, when she takes up a bucket of nuts to Báinin's boggy hill pasture, he comes flying down to meet her, leaping from ridge to ridge of the old lazy-beds. For weeks past, he has been there to saddle within half-an-hour of coming home on the school bus. And now, two months of holiday stretch ahead in a delirium of choice: all that empty shore, all that unfenced mountain.

Should we be more cautious? Should we be worrying that the pony will break into a gallop on the strand or put a foot wrong on the hillside? Would we be less sanguine if we knew more about horses? Probably yes to all these. But I find myself thinking that this was not the best of times at which to be born into the world: let her at least be amazed by her childhood.

Keeping the Peace

THERE IS NO mistaking the sound of an animal in trouble. Just as the bellow for help is like no other shout, so the yell of a terrified beast is like no other voice it has; there is something appalling about it. As Nancy's hysterical bleating brought me running to The Hollow, the ducklings and their mother hen were shrinking together, overwhelmed by the clamour of a goat in distress.

She was lying upside down in the stream — having, by the look of it, tried to leap from one bank to the other while still tethered to a concrete block. The floods have carved the stream bed deeply there, and at any other season she probably would have drowned. As it was, she escaped with a wetting right up to her silky little beard. I unwound the tether from her leg and hoisted her up to the bank, glad she was not the cow in the drain that our neighbours sometimes have to cope with. She trembled for a long while and stood three-legged while we consoled her with an extra feed of barley.

Even on an acre, livestock can demand a lot of attention — especially on an acre, in fact, since the less room they have the more there is to go wrong. Left on the hill, the pony looks after himself; brought down to crop our marginal grass, he leaves a trail of hoof-prints through the newly-sown turnips and ends up in the middle of the strawberry bed. The goats have always to be tethered, and pairs of hollow concrete blocks now lie about at a dozen grassy corners. They are not elegant, but they serve.

We can never be easy now about leaving the homestead unattended, even for an hour or two. When we need to be away at the bog, the goats are tethered carefully in the middle of the hen run, far from any height, hole or protuberance from which they might hang themselves and far enough apart from each other to prevent any fatal entanglement. The knots are checked to make sure that reefs have not turned into grannies. There will come a day, I suppose, when we shall arrive home to find the garden devastated, and then we shall invest in chrome leather collars and chains and swivels.

Having the stock so close about me as I work, whether digging or weeding or, as at the moment, doing both and building a turf shed, means that I possibly interfere in their affairs much more than I should. Were I a proper farmer, driving a grown-up tractor and herding man-size cattle, the squabbles of the farmyard poultry would pass beneath my notice, or at best be sorted out by my wife in quick sorties with a broom. But since, for much of the time, the acre is all my world, I cannot help but get involved.

Take, for example, this feud that has arisen between myself and Fred, the drake. I remember how concerned we were for him when he first arrived: a dapper little bird of distant Indian Runner parentage trying to ingratiate himself with a bevy of bosomy white Aylesburys twice his size. They wanted none of him at first, but hunted him out of their midst with lowered necks. He came back again and again, bobbing his head in propitiation. Eventually, they let him tag along, but played tricks on him — letting him fall asleep beside them and then walking quietly away. Later, of course, when he had made his drakehood plain, they became his adoring and submissive harem.

He has looked after them well, I'll grant him that. He leads them on long foraging expeditions far up the rocky hill above the road and far down through the willow thickets along the stream on Bridie's land, and brings them always safely home by dusk. And, if he should take them on raids through the fence into the hen run, shouldering our layers away from their bowls of mash — well, that was ordinary brigandage and to be expected. "Here comes the Heavy Gang!" we'd say and stand guard until the hens had finished.

No: it is Fred's wanton persecutions that upset me — his onslaughts against any hen that comes within 10 feet, sometimes chasing one the width of the field to seize her neck in his beak and pound her face in the dust like any schoolyard bully. If the hens had a cock to look after them, this would never have started.

At first the squawks from the hen-run would bring my intervention: a bellow in my new stentorian, outdoor voice and perhaps an absurd descent with flapping arms. And sometimes he would, indeed, hesitate in mid-pursuit or even turn and run. But his persistence wore me down; it is up to the hens to stay out of his way.

Now, however, he is going too far in this thuggery, for his latest victim is his only surviving offspring.

Of the first batch of duck eggs we put under a clocking hen this spring, a mere three hatched successfully. Last week, the ducklings seemed big enough to look after themselves, so we returned a none-too-reluctant hen to her own run. The young ducks huddled together outside the wire, peering in after their foster-mother, and here they came each day until two of them disappeared, leaving not a feather behind.

The most likely suspects are the two big tom-cats currently attending our Sooty, but they persist in bland innocence and I am still waiting for the elastic for a catapult. The evidence doubtless lies deep in one of the long, green tunnels between the potato ridges: tunnels that could hold a regiment of predators.

The surviving duckling, meanwhile, keeps her daily vigil at the wire, waiting like a refugee child for a mother who will never come. To arrive at the wire, she has to leave her tea-chest beside the duck house in The Hollow, cross the stream by the wooden bridge, climb the steep steps up the bank, circle the house beneath the kitchen window and pass down by the shadowy mouths of the potato furrows.

But the real gauntlet she must pass is the squadron of big ducks — one of which is her natural mother — and Fred, her father who will beat her up as unmercifully as he would a detested hen. If I hear her anguished squeaking, like that of a rubber duck being punched, I storm down into The Hollow, roaring imprecations and snatching up a stick. Fred runs at once — but knows, unfortunately, that I do not intend to kill him.

Will he ever admit the duckling to his company? Perhaps, if she survives long enough, and as long as she's not a he.

Summer Vintage

THEY HAVE PROMISED to get around to tarring the Corragaun road this year, and I shall be sorry when they do. It will please my neighbours above the lake, of course, whose car springs have suffered so long, and even I should find it pleasant to cycle that way to the strand without jolting over ruts and skidding through drifts of gravel. But something will be lost to the boreen when they tar and tame it. For all these years it has belonged to an outpost of human settlement, carrying its intimate, unhurried traffic in the shelter of close, high hedges. It has been a gentler way for walking when the wind is off the mountain; it has gathered stray cattle; it has funnelled the sheep from the hill to the dipping pen. When it is joined to the rest of the tarmacadamed world, will the hedges seem suddenly to press too close and have to be slashed back? And when the tourists start to blunder that way with caravans in tow, will that little twist below Michael's house — that surprising and fallible little squiggle in the road — will that have to be ironed out?

We were along the hedges of the boreen the other day, picking honeysuckle blossom for summer wine — bucketfuls of heavy-scented trumpets, pink and gold. After the success of our elderflower and blackberry wines, we needed only the recipe to try fermenting the fragrance of this opulent flower. Culpeper, a resourceful if somewhat star-struck herbalist, thought that honeysuckle was "cleansing, consuming and digesting and therefore no way fit for inflammations. Take a leaf and chew it in your mouth and you will quickly find it likelier to cause a sore mouth and throat than cure it. If it be not good for this, what is it good for? It is good for something, for God and nature made nothing in vain."

It is good for wine, if the editor of England's *Amateur Winemaker* can be trusted, responding well to the working of a Sauternes yeast and a dollop of strong tea for tannin (it's the tannin that gives a zest or bite to wines and leaves a pleasant dryness in the mouth.) The challenge in country winemaking, it seems to us, is to find the ingredients which have enough sweetness and real flavour of their own not to need heaping with sugar and pounds of raisins.

Along with the elderflower and honeysuckle, we have also made wine from our gooseberries this summer; later there will be elderberries and the ineffable blackberry. All this begins to take space, and the shelves of the kitchen dresser are now lined with bottles gently working in the warmth from the range (for each bubble, an equal weight of alcohol: what a thought!).

It has also virtually brought to an end our last little bit of spending on "shop" wine, since the kind of plonk we can afford is not a patch on our own produce and is quite likely to give us a headache after only one glass. In due course, we hope, a modest goblet of our wine will become as acceptable to country visitors as the traditional — but now prohibitive — glass of whiskey or syrupy sherry.

An activity in sympathy with wine-making has been our first experiments with cheese (or rather, the first with goat's milk cheese, since Ethna has in her time used Mayo cows' milk, to make a good approximation of Lough Glinn). Now that we have weaned Sally, the kid, to a bottle, there is more milk to spare for such delicacies as Lady Redesdale's Wensleydale cheese: so much for the goat as the "poor man's cow".

It takes a gallon of milk to make a pound of Wensleydale and there is no greater mystique to cheese-making than to following any other kitchen recipe with a few crucial temperatures and timings. Once you have split the milk into curds and whey by using rennet, the rest of the work lies in repeated squeezes of the curds with a 10 lb weight. The cheese has to be turned once a day for three days and it is ripe in three to four weeks.

We have yet to taste goat's butter ("such a superlative product," says David Mackenzie, "that, once it has been savoured, the best of cow's butter becomes, in comparison, uninteresting grease") because the butterfat content of Nancy's pints is too low to make it worthwhile. But we do make yogurt in a Thermos flask and improve even that by letting it drip in butter muslin to produce "hung yogurt," an incomparable addition to any salad.

All dairying demands hygiene as a habit, and the goat's dusty dung can make problems. Most goatkeepers brush their nannies well before milking, and even a hoovering might not come amiss. But we are not that worried about a few coliform bacteria in the milk, given the millions we swallow whenever we clean the goathouse. Nor do we feel we should pasteurise the milk before drinking it.

But there seem to be difficulties ahead for commercial goatkeepers as the demand for their milk increases in the cities and some dirty milk, inevitably, finds its way into the shops. There will be moves towards pasteurisation — a process which, some argue, can destroy its beneficent qualities by changing the proteins. The members of the Irish Goat Club are working hard to produce a scheme for regular testing and Grade A Milk, so that freshness and cleanliness are enough.

Pasteurisation kills living organisms. So do antibotics — but not always in the right kind of way. We are frustrated to find that the only layers' mash we can buy for our hens is laced with antibiotics in the sort of sub-therapeutic dose that does more harm than good.

It is doubtful that it helps the hens, since it is likely to mask any sign of disease and to make the birds drug-resistant. And it could do us harm — not least by giving us the same resistant intestinal flora that the chickens have. If there come a time when we *need* antibiotics, we'd like them to work.

But the drugs seem inescapable as additives to made-up poultry foods. The alternative is to buy separate bags of pollard, bran, crushed oats and bonemeal and make up feed by the quarter ton. Until the potatoes are up and the poyeens come pouring in, we may do just that.

Birds of Passage

ON THE WALL is a picture that I painted nearly twenty years ago, when I lived for a winter in Connemara, across the bay from here. It shows a rough road leading up to the horizon past ricks of turf and the back of a lanky man in cap, Wellingtons and drab raincoat pushing his bicycle up the hill. It is a rather sombre picture, painted in browns and blue-greys and you can tell by the set of the man that he is pushing the bicycle slowly and thoughtfully and will take his time arriving.

Not everybody gets to paint his own destiny, all unknowing. For there I was this week, pushing my bicycle up the bog road on a most unprepossessing day, with the cloud clinging to the mountain like a fungus and a stout east wind pressing down from the sodden brown ridge. As in the picture, there was nobody else in view, and as I plodded past the turf ricks I was asking myself — not unnaturally, perhaps — if I was happy.

And I decided that I must be, because I wasn't looking forward to anything, and also that I had better be because nothing much more wonderful was likely to happen. Both were unfamiliar feelings for someone who had spent much of his life suspended in the present and longing for the future — for the evening, the weekend, the holiday, the letter in the post — that would make all the good things come true.

Now that there is nothing and nobody left to blame for postponing paradise, I am learning, somewhat awkwardly, to enjoy the present. The restrictions of a regular job, the dependence on the city-machine — these could, indeed, be frustrating, but they were also a kind of excuse. They provided a perpetual "if only" by which it became a habit to hang back from trusting the current moment, even when it could have been a good one. Now I have no more alibis for failing to confront the present and being happy in it. The future has arrived.

Thus does the bog induce philosophy. On the back of my bicycle, meanwhile, were lashed two buckets in which I was going to carry stones. One bucket of stones might be thought enough to carry, but two give a better balance.

Ahead of me, at the very end of the bog road, was the mountain river and on the far side of it I could see the dark cairns and dolmens of the turf on our bog. Loyal readers of this chronicle will know the problems the river has made in carrying out turf, whether by donkey or wheelbarrow or the simple bag on the back. But we are nearing a solution by the building of a causeway which will carry a tractor and trailer across the torrent.

A JCB had clawed at the boulders in the riverbed, jockeying the biggest into a rampart across the flow and piling more behind them. Today's job was to fill the holes. The river was swollen from a thunderstorm. It rattled and foamed across the causeway, swirling bronze about the white boulders and squeezing my boots as I waded about. I filled the buckets with stones the size of two fists — small enough to make a surface but big enough to stay put until the next really battering flood. The rain in the wind grew steadily more drenching; it dripped off the peak of my cap as I stooped. There was no point in retreating before I had something to show for the day. So I carried on stone-shifting and I belted out "My Lagan Love" against the roar of the water, knowing I could wail like a lovesick *Leannsidhe* and there was no one for miles to hear.

The next day the sun came out again and there were three flamingoes on the lake.

The news was brought by a summer visitor (himself a rare enough species this year) who had taken his children boating in a rubber dinghy. When they asked him, "Daddy, what are those big pink birds?" he almost capsized with surprise. Flamingoes belong in Africa or on the Mediterranean deltas, or at least in a zoo — not on the wilder shores of Connacht.

By a pleasing coincidence, I have tended to think of the wetlands behind the sand-dunes as "the Camargue" — not because I have been to that celebrated delta of the Rhone but because everything I have seen or read about it seems to conjure the character of our watery local sea-maze: in particular, its brilliance of light and the long fetch of the wind. A few thousand flamingoes were all it needed.

The lake the three birds had chosen was a perfect habitat for them — a large, brackish sheet of water, most of it only ankle-deep. The sea is a few hundred yards away across the strand, but the spring tides — such as we had this week — swirl up to join what has now become a sandy lagoon rather than the deep, freshwater lake it used to be.

When I went down to visit the birds, they had the lake to themselves except for a few indifferent swans and gulls. The pink plumage of the birds caught the eye from half-a-mile away. Constable used to put a dab of red in his trees to make the leaves look greener and there is nothing like flamingo-pink for bringing out the cooler, minty greens of an Irish landscape. The birds positively glowed, pink as roses, as fishing-buoys, as teenage lipstick — and their colour was reflected in the water in soft pink squiggles as they dredged the sand for algae with their bills held upside down.

One of the trio was much larger and more intensely coloured than the others, his neck a deep coral pink. I presumed he was a cock bird, on tour with two wives. It was he who led the retreat when I waded too close: a twenty-yard margin was their limit before they moved off or took to the air like leaping dancers, spreading their wings in a sudden billow of carmine and black and trailing their long legs to a quieter part of the lake.

The last time I saw a flamingo was on a similar seaside lake at Ballycotton, in County Cork, about five years ago. I presumed it had escaped from Dublin Zoo and was flying south. These birds, also, I presume to have escaped (but not from our nearest zoo, at Westport, which doesn't have flamingoes). They seem to have regained their shyness of man, behaving, in fact, just as they do in the Camargue — or even in Chile, where these particular birds may have originated.

Room at the Top

CEZANNE PAINTED HIS Mont Sainte-Victoire sixty times and still was not satisfied. The mountain obsessed him. What Renoir, on a visit, painted as a mere hillock beyond the trees was for Cezanne a looming mass of rock: he dragged it forward from the Provencal horizon and built it up from trembling shards of light.

But I wonder did he ever climb it? Probably not; his energy was in the eye.

Mweelrea, highest peak in Connacht, needs no cubist games with perspective to pull it into our lives. It fills half the window where we sit to eat. And from this month on, as the arc of the sun starts to shorten dramatically and the air clears for winter, we shall dwell increasingly in its presence: a close, dark bulk in the morning, holding back the light, and at evening a mirror to the sunset, its rocky ramparts glowing pink and purple. Mweelrea is *An maol riabhach,* the grey, bald mountain — the Irish for once uninspired to the point of injustice. I prefer *An maol ri,* however unauthentic. And to our daughter the mountain is a monument to Grandad, regally at rest in his armchair.

Until last Sunday, I had not gone up Mweelrea in years. Earlier ascents are woven into memories of weekend expeditions from Dublin, of grubby sleeping bags in mildewed cottages, of raucous sessions in crossroads pubs while the girls finished cooking the curry. It was all very carefree, very Irish, improbably innocent.

Later, more sedately, I climbed the mountain with Ethna, from the bog where we now cut our turf. But since actually coming to live below Mweelrea we have had no time or energy for unproductive exercise. Besides, the mountain now belongs to a more earnest world than that of scrambling up heights for sport. It is the bringer of floods and thunderous gale-gusts. It is the feast and the famine of sheep. To the farmers beneath it, its terrain is as familiar as the meadow outside the door. On the day that I climbed it with Ethna, we met a farmer's wife working with a sheepdog along the high slope under the peak. Her woolly cardigan, flapping in the breeze, did much to demythologise the mountain as a test of endeavour.

Even so, at 2,686 feet, it is still a fair old climb — and a spectacular initiation when one is 11½ years old. I had promised Michele some sort of expedition by the two of us this summer, and as the last days of holiday ticked away with no prospect of a long-awaited camping trip to the islands, I took the gift of a calm, clear day to salvage what was left of my honour.

Mweelrea, to quote Tony Whilde's excellent pocket guide to the walks of the west, "provides a variety of climbing and scenery unsurpassed in the west of Ireland. To describe only one route to the summit would do an injustice to this remote grit and sandstone massif". He goes on to describe five ways up, starting with what is certainly the most exciting approach — by boat across the mouth of the Killary — and proceeding to the dramatic ascents by ridge and corrie from the shadows of Doolough Pass.

Michele and I took the nearest way — through a field with a horse called Jenny and out onto the bog. From there to the peak was a steady, progressively steeper, trudge, with enough proximity to beetling cliffs, massive boulders and slides of scree to furnish the adventure: unless we jumped, we weren't going to fall off anything.

Our daughter's appreciation of landscape and the natural world can seem almost too good to be true. There are times when I am afraid that her enthusiasm is wholly rehearsed from the current adventure of the Famous Five and that secretly she is hankering for discos and junk food. But it is hardly her fault if I find "Yippee!" a little dated, and her delight in the mountain's miniature flowers, the soda-water streams of its little alpine meadows, the revelation of the views from the ridge, could not have been more open-hearted.

Her chief emotion at the summit was one of incredulity at having got there at all. We had arrived in just over two hours, with pauses for picnics until the midges drove us on. Our pace was easy and companionable: the new life has given us both a stamina we can almost take for granted.

We had an eagle's view of Connacht. To the north, beyond Achill, ran the isthmus of Belmullet. To the south-east, through the Twelve Bens, the lakes were spilled like mercury across the dun desert of Connemara, and beyond was Galway Bay and the grey horizon of the Burren — a clear view of fifty miles or more.

As we sat in contemplation, enjoying the last of the frozen

strawberries, we were treated to a strange little episode. The weather was exceptionally calm and fine: on not more than a dozen days in the year could one sit at the top in such silence and comfort. But suddenly, from behind the dark peat hag that marks the actual summit came a rattling, snapping sound, like that of bunting in a stiff wind. As we tried to make sense of it, we saw clods of turf snatched up from the ground and thrown about. Michele clutched at me in fright, and in the moments before the whirlwind veered away over the cliff I, too, could have found it easy to believe in angry elementals; it was an eerie intrusion.

All this time we had the mountain to ourselves, and only a scatter of fresh orange peel at the summit and the prints of climbing boots in the peat were reminders that this was, after all, the holiday season. But as we came down the ridge we exchanged greetings with a group of young people toiling upwards. Michele was horrified to see them. "Daddy!" she hissed. "That orange peel! They'll think it was us!"

Working Arrangements

Ethna writes the next four chapters . . .

PERHAPS IT WAS no wonder that Michael wanted to escape from the holding, even to the extent of going for a 2,000-mile bicycle ride around the island — an extreme example of going for a walk. He must sometimes feel swamped here in a sea of femininity, with 17 hens, five ducks, two goats, a cat, a wife and a daughter. There is very little male back-up in one drake, one tom-kitten and a gelding. He even had to witness the emasculation of Báinín. Things were worse when the bees were here — 150,000 females to a handful of mates, most of whom were flung out before the winter set in.

There are no creatures more female than the hens. Disconcertingly, and indeed with some amusement, I can see among them girls I went to school with, middle-aged aunts, former colleagues of both sexes, other people's mothers, and, if I could see myself as others do, I'm sure I'm there, too. The ducks are much less individual — they are more like the female mob who chanted over their knitting as Marie Antoinette was guillotined — vociferous when attention was centred on others, but ready to scarper, clutching their bundles, if the executioners turned on them. The geese, when they were here, were much more regal — like empresses, their gander was a consort not a monarch. And Sooty has all the femininity of the feline.

Some readers have wondered how I have fared in the rugged existence described weekly in these pages. What kind of life is this for a woman? Where has Women's Lib left me, or where have I left Women's Lib? One fact is paramount: this lifestyle plants us back in the era when, whatever their status, women had not lost their economic role in the family; when they were baker, brewer, creamery manager, food processor, spinner, weaver, tailor, healer, and when men produced the food and raw material.

There was a natural division of labour then between work that needed muscle power and work that merely required endurance — the first mainly outside the house, the second mainly indoors. In summer, enough of her work was outside to give a woman fresh air, and keep her from expiring over a hot stove. For centuries there was no talk of women's liberation because there was no time, nor any great need, for it where work was concerned.

Then both inside and outside work became mechanised and specialised and a great variety of jobs came within the physical competence of women. But then, as men discovered how to use their brains, they cornered that end of the job market and left women with the repetitive and uninteresting jobs both inside and outside the home. When health care was professionalised, men took over the doctoring, leaving the cleaning up to the women. When engineering ceased to require muscle, women were still kept out, and they had to battle their way into both these professions.

You don't take on our kind of life if you want to avoid hard work, but once in, there are very few jobs beyond the physical competence of women, except perhaps turf-cutting — the rest is a matter of fitness. One still has to be wary of the natural tendency of the male to appropriate the interesting jobs. Growing vegetables is more interesting than cleaning them; making a fence is more congenial than cleaning out the henhouse; bricklaying is more satisfying than cleaning up afterwards. Note the repetition of the word *clean* on the distaff side!

It is not a bad idea to make out a rough roster of the jobs that have to be done: the ones he dislikes and you don't mind (watch those); the ones you dislike and he doesn't mind; and the ones you both dislike. An agreed and equitable arrangement should leave no room for resentment, provided the dishwashing gets shared on a continuing basis and not just for the first week.

I have a bad head for heights, so I don't mind holding the ladder while Michael carries out roof repairs. On the other hand, I tend to do the plumbing and he holds the ladder while I squeeze halfway through the trapdoor to the water tank in the roof. You can find yourself in the position of labouring mate to the master craftsman rather than equal partners, and avoiding this demotion calls for eternal vigilance.

Elizabeth West, another "Another Lifer," describes it in her book "Garden in the Hills": "Our work seems to fall into two separate compartments — *his* work and *her* work. For example, *his* work is deciding where the peas shall be sown. *Her* work is digging the trench. *His* work is sorting out the pea canes and netting. *Her* work is filling the trench with compost. *His* work is erecting the canes and netting and sowing the peas and, when they are ready for picking, deciding which pods should be kept for seed and marking them. *Her* work is picking all the other peas and cooking them. At the end of the season *his* work is removing the canes and netting, and throwing them in a heap on the ground. *Her* work is sorting them out, picking off all the bits of pea vine, folding up the nets and putting them away tidily ready for next year.

"I hasten to add that it is only the humdrum labouring that is *her* work. Dramatic labouring (like excavating stormwater trenches) or artistic labouring (like shifting boulders to form rockeries) or essential labouring (like pathway engineering) is most definitely *his* work."

Women's work, more often, is the daily repetition of chores. Relentless routine work, such as animal care, must always be shared — otherwise you never get away for a day or get a morning in bed or the luxury of being ill for a couple of days. You can shackle yourself to a couple of goats by being their only milker because they don't like strangers messing around with them. You've got to make sure he is no stranger to them by doing one week on and one week off; and the same with the cooking, bringing in the turf, dishwashing. On the other hand, you must do your share of the weeding, compost making, turf saving and mucking out.

I love the bog as a once-a-year job. With packed lunch and transistor radio or cassette player, I climb 800 feet up the lower flanks of the mountain. The sea falls away below and the islands have water all around them, unlike the cardboard cutouts they usually resemble on the horizon. I am out of range of interruptions, the larks do their invisible rope trick out of sight above me, the sun warms my shoulders, and there is just enough breeze to keep the flies away.

Most turf work requires little mental effort, so the mind is free. This year I devised the structure and plot of some short stories to write while the turf is burning next winter. I drag myself home bone weary at the end of the day, and next morning I am rested and renewed and more alive than I knew possible.

Having your equality accepted by your neighbours is another day's work, and one that is still in the forenoon of time measured in decades if not in centuries. The male chauvinist is alive and well and undisputed lord of the green fields, airy mountains and rushy glens of Ireland.

Minority View

WITH MICHAEL AWAY on his cycling tour of Ireland, outpedalling Bulfin, while the womenfolk look after the homestead and this column, perhaps the third member of this family should have a chance to say what she thinks of "another life." Some children are more likely than others to be uprooted during schooldays: if their fathers are bank officials, or in the public service or other occupation where promotion means change. (We haven't yet reached the level of sexual equality which would mean that the family could follow mother's job). This mobility usually leads to another town and a better position, and is not to be confused with the impulsive migrations indulged in by Americans. Aunt Mary, visiting us recently from Florida, described the nine moves she has made since she got married. But then Americans are likely to change their houses as often as their cars.

When I was the same age as Michele my family transferred from the countryside to a town, in what social jargon refers to as upward mobility. This kind of move was regarded as unquestionably right because it had an accepted logic. We are conscious that one day we may be called on by our daughter to account for our outward-bounding if life gets too much for her and exciting times are rumoured in the city.

On our side of the hill there are three other families with children who have returned here from England and the U.S.A., and in the parish I am sure there are another dozen. One family has already experienced teenage revolt against "this dump" and "why did we ever leave the city to come here?" But that may be the endemic discontent of teenagers.

Just now Michele would say that it was the most wonderful place on earth, because on Sunday she competed in her first horse race. Killadoon race committee punctuated the holidays by having the strand races on the day before school re-opened. For weeks the idea hovered around that she might let Báinín try his paces in a pony race with someone else in the saddle. But in this busy season nobody had time to lunge him, and in his present half-trained state he was likely to

Wild and Free

REFERENCES BY US to "our side of the hill" have given many readers the idea that we are very isolated. Visitors this summer were surprised to find our nearest neighbours a couple of hundred yards away. From the bend where the road winds around the hill, unfolding a panorama of white sands, ocean, island and mountains, to the Silver Strand, where it ends, is four miles.

In the last century this outpost of the Congested Districts lived up to that description. When Lord Lucan cleared the tenants off the lands of Thallabawn around 1850, there were 300 families on that stretch of roughly 2,500 acres of farmland. Now there are thirty occupied houses, of which nineteen are in our direct line of vision. Most of the houses here have been built on sites that command a view of a fine selection of neighbours.

Looking into the next county we can also see the white stitching of houses along the strands and rugged cliffs of Lettergesh, across the Killary in Galway to the south, and further west the clustered villages of Tully. Renvyle House Hotel is a focal point which defines geographically the other houses marching out along the headland. And on a clear day we can see the lobster ponds and the village of Aughrisbeg, west of Cleggan and fifteen miles away as the crow flies.

If we need more reassurance of surrounding humanity, twelve miles to the south-west we pick out the houses of our friends in East End, Inishbofin; or swing around due west and count the villages on Inishturk, eight miles offshore and ten away from us. In this kind of landscape, strategically placed on the edge of the Atlantic seaboard, the feeling of being part of a wider world comes naturally. It is not alone the wide horizons and the peephole views of distant mountain ranges, glimpsed between our own lofty peaks; we are also linked to faraway places by the daily passing jets, which leave their vapour trail in the stratosphere, heading for the next landfall from us in North America; and, until recently, by the annual spring visits of Continental trawlers, lighting up the empty spaces of the western approaches.

The narrow road which serves this area stops on the map halfway down the hill. But for many years now the track which continued to the Silver Strand has been tarred, and future mappers may well include it. The mile-long loop road, which links the townland of Corragaun to this main highway, was made of sand and gravel until, one fine September day just past, the yellow County Council trucks arrived with chips and smoking tar and bustling purposeful men to lay a hard top on it like a strip of carpet. But the half-mile length of boreen, which branches from it to the sea, mercifully escaped their ministrations.

I hold no brief for sand and gravel roads. Like a war veteran, I carry shrapnel from one in my knee — grains of sand embedded there, legacy of youthful falls off bicycles. But Báinín prefers them — he can pick his unshod steps around the stones and on the grassy sides — and tarring seems to change the atmosphere and environment of a byway.

This particular boreen is everything a country lane should be: a spring and summer festival of wild flowers, terraced on the ditches and hiding in the drains, a refuge for the birds and the few wild mammals we have here, and an autumn cornucopia of blackberries, sloes, rosehips and hazelnuts. A rocky mound on one side, a *creagán*, has saved the natural ecology, while the fields around were cleared of rocks and drained.

I wonder if the comparative economics show that the advantages of reclaiming it would be greater than the value of its wild harvest. It produces enough vitamin C to keep the thirty local families in robust health for a year; enough fruit and flowers to satisfy their needs in jams and wines; herbs for teas and remedies; nectar for the honeybee; horsetail for scouring pots and pans; reeds and sally rods for weaving into baskets; roots and lichens to dye their wool; and nuts, at least enough for Hallowe'en.

So far, no slurries poison the streams and watercourses, and the best side of this lane is out of the reach of silage effluent. The neighbouring fields are not sprayed with chemical weedkillers or insecticides, but if agricultural "progress" catches up with this corner of the west, and it might, there is no way that this boreen to the sea could be saved. Few voices would be raised against neighbours polluting streams and watercourses running straight into the sea. Unfortunately, the death of a boreen would happen so slowly that I fear it would cause no outcry. So far it is safe, and long may it stay that way.

While we are busy harvesting the wild and free fruits of the hedgerows, the produce of our own acre is slowly finding its way into barn and freezer. One windy and sunny day recently our neighbour Michael crossed the ditch with his scythe to stand in for our own wandering reaper and cut the barley. (I can turn my hand to most jobs, but would fear for the safety of my legs if I took a scythe in my hands).

We raced against the weather forecast and pregnant clouds piling up across Killary and spilling over on to the flanks of Mweelrea. I tied the sheaves while Michael cut, and we stacked them not in stooks, because of the broken weather, but in cocks like hay, with the dry grain heads towards the centre, and covered them with bags tied down. The rood was cleared before the first big drops heralded two days of rain; and I took my aching bones back to the household chores.

Another if unwelcome harvest this year is a phenomenal growth of chickweed. Since August it has been inexorably encroaching between and over everything in the garden like a green foam tide. I give it to the hens and to the goats and pile it on the compost heap, and still it persists. Several of our books, of the living off nature type, recommend it as an excellent salad with dandelion leaves, and one says that the young leaves, when boiled, can hardly be distinguished from spring spinach and are equally wholesome.

Mrs Grieve's "Modern Herbal" (modern in 1931!) cannot say too much for chickweed as a demulcent ointment, a poultice for external abscesses. As a decoction, it is good for constipation, as an infusion for coughs and hoarseness, or use the juice for redness in the face, and eat it raw for obesity. But it does nothing for the backache got in fighting it.

Goat Games

IN THE DAYS when windows were smaller and lights were dimmer, the bright March sunshine illuminated dusty corners and, like an electronic beam, activated housewives to the great catharsis of spring cleaning. As this usually took place before Easter, Holy Week recalls to many of us a mixture of paint and palm leaves, dust and incense. Nowadays this vernal explosion of activity is spread more evenly over the year. Only parts of the country, where the Stations have survived, can now produce a household convulsion of the same magnitude.

The Stations are an historical commemoration of a time when churches were few and travel difficult, and the parish priest went twice a year to say Mass in houses in isolated areas. On our side of the hill every house has the Stations once every 15 years, which provides a not unwelcome occasion to redecorate and refurbish the home. It is now a neighbourhood festival, social as well as religious, particularly when it is held in the evening and the traditional meal is followed by singing and dancing. Our neighbours, Joe and Kathleen, have just had the Stations and are now recovering from weeks of hectic activity which culminated in a gargantuan feast preceded by Mass and followed by a dance for the thirty-odd families in the station area and their own nearby relations.

Like spring cleaning, the Stations are dominated by women. Under their command, the house is turned inside out, recesses and presses are excavated, surfaces painted, floor coverings renewed, new curtains are hung. Men are commissioned to carry out repairs, improve streets and yards, and make innumerable journeys to the town for materials. Closer to the date, poultry are plucked, a lamb slaughtered and hams are bought, cakes are baked and desserts prepared.

With the house and the food at the peak of her demanding perfection, the Stations are a personal triumph for the housewife in the eyes of the neighbours, although those same neighbours are already well acquainted with the house itself and its hospitality. Comes the day and the women still have pride of place. Forming the core of the gathering they sit inside the cleared livingroom, while the men stand on the fringes and overflow into the hall and out on to the street. It is an important cultural occasion as much as a Christian celebration. The modern trend to have the Mass in the church, with no subsequent feast, is an erosion of culture.

With the first cutting edge of easterly wind slicing down from the hill, I was glad we had our new goats home and acclimatised before the worst excesses of winter on the western seaboard. They came from Wicklow and the shelter rather than the exposure of mountains. Contrary to commonly-held belief, the goat is not the hardy animal suggested by its natural mountain habitat and its predilection for climbing.

In the wild herds, goats make comfortable sleeping quarters, which they keep on a permanent basis, and they have a range of temporary shelters mapped out over their foraging terrain — like most animals, they dislike wind and wet.

The two new goats, inheriting the names of Nancy and Sally, are white, hornless and dignified. At first acquaintance they showed none of the puckish temperament of their proletarian predecessors, who were the epitome of caprine *capriccio* — a pair of lovable rascals given to playful butting, fore and aft, when you bent down to their level. The new Nancy and Sally appeared characterless by comparison. But after a few days, as they got to know their domain, their natural friskiness emerged. Now they race each other to high vantage points when they are being led out to browse, dragging me at a less dignified pace than I would choose; or they prance about winding their leads around my legs and turning the short stroll into Charlie Chaplin act.

Goats are very social animals, and if they have not got goat companions, they demand human companionship in a most importunate manner. Sally, the kid, has been weaned long ago off her mother, but given half a chance she is back there at the milk bar for a quick snack. They have to be kept close enough to commune, yet not so close as to allow Sally to regress.

David Mackenzie was the great goat behavioural expert, and his book, *"Goat Husbandry"*, is the definitive work on their management. The relationship between you and your goats is either one of acceptance as one of their own species or as an outside threat.

The goat handler is cast by them in one of the roles in the social structure of the wild flock.

"The king billy of the flock rules by right of strength and courage . . . but shares the practical leadership of the foraging expedition with an old she-goat, the flock queen, who is the mainspring of the life of the flock. When she stops to feed, the flock feeds, when she raises her head from browsing and stares at the billy, the king moves on to the next foraging site.

"When man enters the social circle of the goat flock he (or she) assumes the rank of kid, flock queen or king billy, according to the circumstances. As kid, man can lead the flock. . . There is no great difficulty in getting into the social circle of the goat's confidence; the difficulty arises in getting in and out at your convenience and still exercising control."

I don't know which role I have been cast in by Nancy and Sally. The nanny, Nancy, is surely a natural for queenship of the tiny flock of two, so while I try to lead them on their foraging expeditions, I expect I'm the billy. That accounts for the total disdain for my leadership shown by Nancy as she stops to nibble the fuchsia hedge on our way down the garden path, and for her immovability until she decides she's had enough. I suppose I should wait until she gives me the nod to move on.

At milking time I can be, briefly, a kid, but I have to be as efficient a milker as one, otherwise I'll be sent packing with a swift kick. The other morning she thought that I was overlong messing around, and she kicked over a bucket of foamy, creamy milk.

This dual casting would seem to work, and I hope that there is small danger of having to carry the billy-goat role to the extent of having to defend my kingship against a real billy — unless the mating season attracts a real, horned, feral puck down from the fastnesses of Mweelrea.

A Yard of Badger

I KNEW I WAS home again when I found myself skinning a badger instead of digging the potatoes, roofing the turf shed or getting on with any of the other urgent works awaiting my return. Life here seems to offer these distractions and we seize them in a sort of defiant celebration of the fact that our time is now our own.

There was, after all, no pressing need for a badger skin. We already had one, in fact, now somewhat motheaten, which Ethna's father had cured in Cavan half-a-century ago. We were not planning to make badger-hair paint-brushes, trout flies or pampooties (though that, now I have thought of it, is not a bad idea).

No, I could have left the poor beast where I found it on my trip to the post office. It was lying on the verge at the top of the hill with its eyes glazed and bright bead of blood on its nose. But the car that had broken its neck in the night had tossed it aside quite unmarked: the long black-and-white coat had the spring and immaculate gloss of a well-fed wild animal all ready for winter. To let it be torn apart by passing dogs seemed quite unthinkable.

Besides, it was the very first badger I had seen in the round, so to speak. Since our move from Dublin, I had met stoat and hedgehog, rat, rabbit, hare and shrew. And our daughter had watched an otter bounding along beside the stream where it runs through Bridie's land. Now, just when I was giving up hope that our bare and windy hillside might shelter anything as big as a badger, here was this elegant, strokeable corpse — a young female, by the look of it — lying in the shadow of a dry-stone wall.

As I hoisted her behind me on the bicycle and turned back home, I reflected on the irony of discovering a badger on my doorstep when I had seen so little wildlife all the way around Ireland. It was one of the hopes of my journey that, travelling quietly along the back roads and by-ways, I might now and then encounter the unexpected. But for all the lack of human activity in the countryside, its mammals remain shy and nocturnal as ever. I did glimpse the red deer of Glenveagh, in County Donegal, as distant heads among the bracken. But the only creature I surprised was a bird, a sparrowhawk: as I whizzed down a steep hill near Glencolumbkille it found itself flying a collision course and in a last-second manouvre swooped *under* the road, through a culvert.

Skinning a freshly-killed animal is not all that difficult, or even especially smelly. It may need some resolution to confront an unfamiliar anatomy, and a heavy, sharp-pointed hunting knife is a help both to skill and confidence.

Turning the animal on to its back, you decide where the zip-fasteners would go if you were planning to put the pelt on again, and then make the cuts by lifting the skin on the point of the knife and running the blade away from you. If you stick it in the guts, *then* it could get smelly.

My previous experience was with sheep and rabbits, both of which can be eased out of their pelts by pushing your fingers (and with the sheep, your fist) as a wedge beneath the skin. The badger would not be parted from her hide so easily. It took me an hour to pare it away from her and my skill stopped short of keeping the nose and claws attached. But at least there were no holes and not a hair out of place on a handsome three feet of flat badger. Now it must be scraped free of fat and cured with salt and alum.

"Can you eat badger?" my daughter wondered, as she watched the bare carcase emerging and looking every bit as wholesome as that of a lamb. The answer in this case had to be no: there is too much phosphorus poison set down around the farms this rat-plagued autumn to take chances on an experiment. But without that special risk, I should not have hesitated in cooking at least a haunch of it.

Cameron's *"Wild Foods of Great Britain"*, first published in 1917, says that badger hams cured by smoking "are a decided delicacy, and may then be cooked and eaten either hot or cold. They are thus commonly treated in Germany, and to a less extent in Ireland," Judy Urquhart, in *"Living Off Nature,"* says that badger ham is supposed to taste even nicer than pork. But Brian Plummer, the biology teacher who writes mildly outrageous books about the British countryside, reported most unfavourably on badger in *"Adventures of An Artisan Hunter."* He found it "disgusting — a cross between oily port and swan droppings". Hedgehog, heron and fox pleased him no better, but feral tomcat was "delicious" and indistinguishable from rabbit.

I would still like to try badger for myself.

In the weeks I was away on my journey, four farm dogs hereabouts had to be shot for sheep-killing and it is still not sure that we have seen the last of it. Only this week, sudden unexplained swirls of bunching and running among the sheep on the hill sent Joe and Peter and their sons hurrying up the fields with shotguns. They found nothing, but the unease persists.

The first pair of dogs killed six ewes at the mountain river and were tracked home along the ridge as they sent one flock after another into turmoil. Since the owner of a killer dog is expected to shoot it and to pay, perhaps, £15 or £20 for a dead ewe, the confrontations between men who know each other can sometimes be traumatic. Although a "good" dog can be led astray by another, there is always the implication of negligence, of dogs kept too hungry or left too much to themselves. Before a man is told that his dog is worrying sheep, identification has to be very sure.

My own skirmishes with farm dogs on the bicycle this autumn left toothmarks in my boots and a new hardness in my heart; any dog that goes for me is going to get kicked, and that's that.

But my neighbours think I could have fared worse. In the old days hereabouts, they tell me, the menace to the cyclist was not so much the dogs as the ganders in the roadside flocks of geese. They would rush at a cyclist with flapping wings and jabbing beak. In one incident still recalled, a lady was thrown over her handlebars when a gander missed his stride and stuck his neck through her rear wheel.

A Two-Fisted Milker

FOR MANY YEARS of my working life, half-past five in the evenings was the time to put on my coat, pick up my briefcase and head off to catch the bus home. When I picture this now, I can see the oily glitter of wet pavements in Westmoreland Street and feel the icy shock of the wind that waited beyond the lee of the Ballast Office. But the Ballast Office is demolished and my evening routine has changed. Half-past five is now the time when I go to milk the goat.

It made sense to share the daily milking, if Nancy could be persuaded to accept two different sets of hands at her udder. The evening milking clashed with cooking dinner. And if Ethna alone had the knack in her fingers and the necessary rapport with the goat, what would happen if she got flu or had to travel to a funeral or even (to admit the unthinkable) insisted on breakfast in bed? So it is she who wraps up warmly at half-past seven each morning and picks her way cautiously across the frosty foot-bridge, while I take her place — still most inexpertly — at the other end of the day.

For a start, there are so many things to carry: two separate buckets of feed, one of lukewarm drinking water, the empty pail for the milk, the tub of udder cream, the flannel wrung out in hot water and disinfectant (with which to wipe the udder without paralysing the goat) and the 12-volt flashlamp. All these can, in fact, be carried on one journey, if someone else opens the door.

Dusk falls slowly here on the open Atlantic coast. Long after the sun has dropped into an inky rim of cloud at the horizon, the afterglow lingers above the islands. I step out to a cyclorama of deep, smoky blue. But down in The Hollow it is already dark and the goats begin to bleat impatiently as they see the flashlamp approaching.

There is quite a mixed community lodging in the shed these nights. Nancy and Sally, her kid, take up most of it, sleeping on an ever-deepening mattress of rushes and spoiled hay. The ducks still roost at one end, pending construction of new quarters, and they have now been joined by the Christmas goose, who was finding her tea-chest lonely and persisted in tagging along when the ducks went to bed.

And finally there is Sooty, the cat, who has taken up residence in the warmest corner, under Nancy's hay box. Since she was banished from the kitchen to keep her away from the dairying, we can only salute her effrontery in finding a bed within inches of Nancy's udder. In folklore, it was the hare that suckled the cow by night; we have heard nothing so kinky about cats and goats.

Once Nancy's nose has reached the dairy nuts, a certain urgency creeps into my movements. When she was delivered to us from the Wicklow Hills this autumn, her owner expressed the hope that we were fast, two-fisted milkers "because Nancy stands still only while she's eating." Indeed, as she chases the last nut around the bottom of the bucket, her rear, offside leg begins to twitch. A few seconds later, if the milk pail has not been snatched up, one dainty but shitty hoof has been plunged into it.

The milking is, therefore, a race against time — particularly since Ethna caught me upping the ration of nuts to buy myself a few extra minutes of stillness. But nothing of my inner turmoil must be communicated to Nancy: panic and curses will make her nervous (and set the ducks gabbling hysterically in the shadows). No — she must be petted and crooned to and her udder (or elder, as I am learning to call it) wiped down as if there were all the time in the world; only then will her teats be full and flowing.

There were nights at the beginning when I was sure I would never learn to milk with both hands at once. The goat's teat requires a special, two-part squeeze which can seem as difficult as the fingering of the uillean pipes and again and again the milk has gone spurting up my sleeve. But there are more nights now when the knack and the rhythm coincide and a great calm descends within the shed as the two jets of milk converge, foaming in the pail.

As I crouch there on the rushes in a golden cave of light, I listen to the sounds around me — the hiss of the milk, the rumbling in one of Nancy's stomachs, the *sotto voce* debate among the ducks, the rattle of the stream outside, and perhaps the night wind moaning — and I sometimes (but not too often) think of the No. 25 bus still inching up the quays, its windows fogged and weeping with the breath of a thousand sighs.

Autumn is the usual time for mating goats, and we do need to get young Sally in kid so that she will be milking when her mother goes dry. But we feel she is still a little small, and intend to wait until

February before taking her 50 miles across the mountains to the nearest pedigree Saanen billy. Meanwhile, we have to hope that no whiff of our goats' presence will drift on the wind to the enormous, shaggy puck who is lodging with a farmer a mile up the hill.

We have no idea of his breed. "He's a Charolais!" jokes the farmer, pointing to the ochreous colour of his prodigiously tangled coat. But while somebody went to the trouble of having him dehorned, he last changed hands for £40, bought by a farmer in the hills near Westport who was told that a good, strong puck would graze down the briars on his land.

His sojourn here is to service the only other goats in the locality besides our own. One was wished on the farmer by friends in Tipperary, who found her coming down the stairs from the children's bedroom and decided enough was enough. Another was found as a kid beside the road along Killary Harbour and is presumed to be an orphan of the feral goats of the mountains. Each is only half the size of Nancy, but they have made enough of a harem for the puck to set him dancing on his hind legs for days.

We had never been close to a billy goat before and so had never smelled the distinctive scent that has got all goats a bad name. At the time of his rutting, it had penetrated even the farmer's house. It is actually the product of the billy's musk glands, behind the horns, and he spreads it around by rubbing his head off his females. We did not smell it at its worst, but, like the farmer, couldn't quite think what it reminded us of: a sweet, acrid odour that might have been silage, gunpowder, the lees of wine and yet was not any of these.

To Ethna, the smell recalled a year in her youth when she worked in New York, mixing perfumes. One of her precious ingredients, which gave the scent body and made it last on the skin, was extracted from the musk glands of the civet cat.

Earthworks

YEARS AGO, in the time of gregarious weekending in the West, one of our number was a work-study engineer with a passion for building dams. Arriving at the cottage in Connemara, he would lead us out with spades to a nearby strand and get us to help him block the course of one of the streams that ran to the sea — this for the simple pleasure of watching a lake build up behind the dam and the ultimate destruction when the tide came in. It was therapy of a kind and, licensed by his eccentric inspiration, we were quite content to be sandcastling children again.

It was another engineer who climbed down into our stream this week to advise me on the embankment I must build to stop the floods undermining the house; their encroachment, he agreed, was becoming "very serious". Leaping from boulder to boulder in his good shoes, he became frankly wistful about the project. "I'd love a job like that," he said. "I never actually get to do anything."

There is certainly something about construction work involving untamed, running water that touches a primordial enthusiasm in man. This year, I have been getting more than my share of it. There was the making of a cistern to trap a hillside stream and the building of a causeway across the mountain river to our cutting on the bog. Now I had to build about six yards of wall, made three feet thick with rocks and concrete, to stop the water taking any more great bites from the steep bank next to our gable.

The alternative was to divert the stream. Scarcely had our friendly engineer departed than there came an offer by telephone of sections of massive sewer pipe, each twelve feet long and five feet across. They were factory "seconds," but quite good enough to turn our torrent aside.

It was a very generous proposal. But I shrank at the thought of trying to manipulate these great pipes without the help of a costly crane. And besides, for all the worry the stream has given us from time to time, I would hate to banish it into a tunnel and lose the sparkle of life it brings to the hollow beside the house.

Even without the piping, of course, it would be possible to cut a new bed for the stream that would steer it further away from the gable bank. A JCB could do it in a morning, my neighbour Michael was urging, and what was scooped out from one place could be dumped in another and save me building any wall "because, with all due respects, one man with a pickaxe has no business taking on a river."

We walked the land to see how the JCB might be led to The Hollow, first across Bridie's field, then through the fence into the hen run, a U-turn round the gully, through another fence and on along the ditch across the strawberries, raspberries and blackcurrants. "Wouldn't do a bit of harm," said Michael.

There was a lot of merit in his scheme. The new cutting would bypass the sharp left-hand bend that had set the stream swirling so destructively in the first place. It would put the willow tree, with its tough bastion of roots, between the gable bank and the water. And it would save me having to heave quite so many rocks about, to say nothing of mixing and pouring several tons of concrete. But the idea foundered on a point of quantity surveying. There would not be half enough material from the new excavations to fill the old watercourse and restore the bank: we should be left with gaping craters.

Committed finally to building the wall, I appointed Ethna to her usual post of clerk of works. She ordered a ton of cement from Louisburgh and alerted the neighbourhood gravel haulier to watch the tides for the right size of shingle. He will arrive in his tractor any day now with a load of wet beach, salt-smelling and garnished with seaweed.

The townland's source of sand is similarly providential. The *duach* — the dunes between the lake and the sea — is robbed endlessly to lime the soil, to hold down the covers on pits of silage and to mix concrete. My neighbour Joe was going that way with his tractor, to take a ram to his ewes on the cliffs beyond the dunes. He left me to work away with a shovel while he set off on foot with the ram. It galloped round him in wild circles on its tether, but was finally persuaded to pursue a distant whiff of ewe.

In the event I was not left to confront the river alone. Michael's son Mick is working with me in the canyon below the gable. We have not waited for the shingle from the beach but have started by using the stream's own gravel in the concrete packed around the foundation boulders.

Before the big floods of the past few years, the stream came splashing through The Hollow between scores of boulders, many of them weighing a couple of hundredweights. Now most of them have been swept away downstream, so that Mick and I have been manhandling the survivors from one end of The Hollow to the other.

No one who has not set out to fill a big hole with rocks can imagine the quantities that are needed. The bed of the stream is now picked clean, as if it were a man-made canal, and I am trundling the wheelbarrow in ever-increasing circles, stealing rocks from ditches and walls. We have even been out into Bridie's land, to carry away the pieces of great sunken boulder shattered by gelignite years ago but never cleared.

In two days, we have raised half the wall a couple of feet. The other half has to wait for a lull in the Atlantic depressions that keep the stream so full. I had tried to shut out the water with sandbags, timber and concrete blocks. But a few hours of rain overnight were enough to sweep it aside, swilling out the sandbags and whisking the timber away.

Mick's father comes over the ditch, flanked by his three dogs, to inspect the work as it progresses. He did, after all, work on the mighty dyke that keeps the sea out of Skegness, and on the best disposition of rocks and concrete there is no one whose word I would rather have.

He is shocked by the change in the stream's behaviour. "I've been watching it for fifty years," he says, "and it never went wild like this." But we both know the reason for the rapid floods that are starting to tear chunks from the mountains, never mind the odd chew at a house. While overgrazing of the hills continues, abetted and encouraged by the Government's sheep headage subsidies, there is nothing to keep the rain where it belongs.

Along the Tide

ABOUT SIX MILES to the north of us, where the sea sweeps round the corner into Clew Bay, a side road arrives at Roonagh Quay, point of departure to Clare Island and Inishturk. It is a lonely cleft in the cliffs; nobody lives there and the quay is usually deserted unless a boat has come out from the islands. This year, at last, the county council has made it more of a proper staging post, with a transit shed for the islanders' goods and a walled enclosure for their cattle and sheep. When I arrived at the quay, four ewes were huddled in a corner, waiting for a boat.

I have had some memorable voyages from Roonagh. It was from here that we sailed out into the mist for an October honeymoon on Clare Island and, later, to a camping holiday among the lonely crosses of Caher. But now, one day in each winter month, it is where I start to walk the shore, looking for dead birds along the tideline.

The national Beached Bird Survey, organised in Ireland by An Foras Forbartha, uses the mortality of seabirds to check on spillages of oil. I am one of about 80 volunteers who make the monthly march and fill in record cards for processing in Dublin. Over the past three winters, the survey has shown Irish waters to be relatively free from oil pollution: in northern Europe, only Norway has such a clean coastline.

All seabirds are beautiful, even in death, and those of the North Atlantic have a spare, streamlined durability that makes their stranding on the tide even more touching. On this coast they are rarely oiled but arrive in immaculate plumage, eyes still bright, as if they had folded their wings to die only a second ago. As I stroke the breast feathers or spread a wing to admire its construction, I seem to feel for a moment the immensity of wind and ocean for which they were designed.

My "beat" on the Atlantic coast brings me birds that one would normally never see close to — puffins and fulmars, kittiwakes and guillemots (and once, as a rarity, the little auk, no bigger than a starling). But on this, the first patrol of winter, there were no dead birds at all. Mortality rises to a peak in February, unless severe gales or oil spills intervene. I had to be content with the novelty of immigrant land birds — fieldfares and redwings in the fields along the shore.

The patrol brings me to a stretch of coastline well away from our own sandy doorstep, so that the sea has had time to make changes from one December to the next. Its encroachments are sometimes so dramatic that I find it hard to accept that they have been going on at much the same rate for centuries.

Starting south from Roonagh, for example. one sets off comfortably on an old, gravelled boreen at the edge of the cliff. But just around the corner, the way is now so undermined as to be near collapse, bringing the old road to an end even more abrupt than it was already. On the shingle beach beyond, I pick a way across greasy black outcrops of peat and find a root of bog oak, a sculpture to bring home. So here, amid today's plastic jetsam and a slippery tangle of kelp, is an ancient forest. Where was the tideline when this oak was growing — a hundred yards distant, or a mile?

The sea goes on chewing away, year by year, at low clay cliffs and raw edges of turf. But it has also thrown up great obstacles against its own advance — ridges of shingle a mile or more long, piled twenty feet high to the peak of equilibrium, so that one teeters and clatters along the top as if walking the pointed ridge of a roof.

No local man would put such penance on himself as to trudge these sliding stones, or take off wellingtons and socks — as I sometimes have to do — to wade the freezing, bog-brown rapids where the moorland river meets the sea. And yet, while I have never actually met another beachcomber on these hikes, any worthwhile piece of jetsam is marked or carried off as soon as it lands ashore. I know of a barn that is crammed to the rafters with ropes, nets, buoys and timber spars. It belongs to an old man who farms by the sea and simply cannot resist adding to his hoard, even though he makes no use of it.

I understand him perfectly; my own collection of ropes and buoys goes on growing with only the vaguest of intentions. But the prize from this week's walk, apart from my bog-oak sculpture, was a large fish-box in purple plastic. We have an endless need for durable containers, and as a receptacle for harvesting potatoes, a purple plastic fish-box will do even better than the pink baby bath, which has split.

Staff of Life

WHEN THE LATE John Lennon first baked a loaf of bread, he found it one of the most uplifting experiences of his life — or so someone was saying on the radio last week. I can certainly vouch that something profound and elemental stirs in the breast of man turned baker. My first new-minted batch of loaves, golden-brown and steaming on their wire tray, were some of the noblest creations ever to come from my hand. But along with the pride, the near-mystical thrill of achievement, went the simple discovery that baking bread is easy.

So it is that when male visitors from Dublin enthuse over slices of our wholemeal, praising its rich flavour and chewy, nutty texture, I encourage them to make the baking of the family bread their special contribution to household health and happiness. The chances are, after all, that their wives are already working to capacity, outside and inside the home, and that regular baking of bread could add one kitchen chore too many. In a marriage of any equality, it should not be remarkable that the husband (the "breadwinner", as it was once safe to call him) should actually make the bread. This will not prevent him from a quiet boasting at dinner parties, prolonging the soup course until the bread platter has been emptied twice at least.

For the husband who is tempted to make baking his thing, his dependable kitchen performance, I will now describe a process of incredible simplicity which takes about 35 minutes to complete, plus the putting in and taking out of the oven. It will produce half a dozen 1½ lb loaves, which is as many as the average oven will hold. These last our family about five days and keep perfectly fresh in the freezer.

The flour we use is special because it is natural — stone-ground, wholemeal flour milled by the monks of Mount Joseph Abbey at Roscrea and sold as Abbey or Howard's. Our local grocery store gets it for us at a little over £8 for a 25 kilo bag. The finished 1½ lb loaf costs us about 20p (counting 5p as the cost of the turf burned to bake it), compared with 35p for two pounds of sliced, plastic pap.

Begin by announcing that you are baking and do not want people coming in and out of the kitchen making draughts (cold draughts can

stop your dough from rising properly). Assemble three mugs and a big jug of water warmed to blood heat. Into each mug you put two level teaspoons of dried yeast (bought in a tin from a wholefood shop) and about a tablespoon of the lukewarm water. Put the mugs somewhere warm for the yeast to "prove", or fizz up.

While the yeast is proving, put two pounds of flour in a big bowl and sprinkle with half a teaspoon of salt. Fetch out your baking tins and grease the insides with margarine to stop the bread sticking.

When the yeast has risen, which takes 10-15 minutes, pour one of the mugs into the flour in the bowl, stir it around with a wooden spoon and add five naggins of the lukewarm water (or 25 fluid ounces or three-quarters of a litre, depending on how your jug is calibrated). Stir until all the flour is wet. Then knead it for five or ten minutes. We do this with a Kenwood mixer and a dough hook. If you're doing it the hard way, turn the mixed dough out on a floury table, knead it with floury hands and use more flour to stop it sticking to you — "wash" your hands with flour, not water.

Wholemeal dough doesn't get elastic in the same way as white flour dough, so just give it the ten minutes of kneading, by which time it will look a bit whitish. Split the lump of dough between two baking tins, half each, and put them somewhere warm with a tea-towel over them. Then deal with the next mug of yeast.

The dough will take 30-40 minutes to rise to fill the tins — more if your kitchen is cold or draughty. During this time, heat the oven to 400 degrees. You can make even better bread by "popping" the risen dough with your fingers and letting it rise again, but we usually don't bother. Put the tins into the oven without banging them, which could make the dough collapse. Since the six tins will take up two shelves in the oven, it is a good idea to switch the bottom ones to the top halfway through the baking and get the loaves evenly brown.

They should be baked in 35-40 minutes. You can test one by turning it out of its tin on to a tray. If the bottom of the loaf is mid-brown, not pale biscuit, and sounds sort of hollow when you tap it with your fingers, it is probably done.

This is the simplest kind of wholemeal bread, baked in the simplest way. It is a superlatively satisfying food. When you get bored with the ease and certainty of making it, there are scores of different kinds of bread — plain, sweet and fancy, sprinkled with sesame seeds, stuffed with bananas or whatever — awaiting your experiment.

All Due Modesty

WHEN THE TOWNSMAN comes to live in the country, there there are few things so mortifying to his sense of sophistication as making silly mistakes about animals and sex. Thus, for some long time after moving to Mayo, I was likely to remark that the cow bellowing so persistently down in Michael's byre must be missing her calf — as if I knew nothing about the agitation of animals in season. I had already identified as a neighbour's bull an ordinary, perhaps slightly overgrown bullock. And at the last Westport horse fair, I was still confusing fillies and colts because I was too shy to stoop down for a proper look.

The countryside is, in some respects, less "earthy" than it was a few decades ago. Certainly there is far less copulation on view and conversation about it has become more scientific. Most cows are no longer taken to a bull but are visited instead by the A.I. technician with his plastic sleeve. Farm stallions are few and far between. Pigs now procreate to order in the recesses of overheated slurry factories. Mountain sheep are about the last farm animals living more or less as God intended, and they conduct their November trysts at a decorous distance up the hill (which is why, on some farms, the ram is daubed on the chest with coloured raddle so that he marks the ewes he tups).

When it came to locating a billygoat to mate with our maiden goatling, Sally, we had to look fifty miles away, to Headford in County Galway, to find a puck of the proper breed. The native Irish "scrub" goat is now scarce enough, but the modern dairy breed (such as our Saanens, which originated in Switzerland) is still an exotic novelty in these parts.

A goat comes into season every three weeks from about August until February, calling with a piercing bleat for most of a day or more and wagging her tail as a small child waves a flag. By this month, we had Sally's date predicted on the kitchen blackboard and had recruited an obliging neighbour with an extra-large boot to his car. Sally was installed on a mattress of hay, with the boot propped open an inch of two for air. She travelled placidly, bleating only when we stopped.

Our destination was a thatched farm-house on a back road in rather wistful country at the edge of the plain of Muigheo, mazed with ivied limestone walls, that feels as if man has lived there for a long, long time. There, Sally, was introduced to Sovereign, a young billy of callow but princely mien.

His interest in Sally was immediate but, to my surprise, was mostly expressed in butting games. Again and again, he reared up on his hind legs to deliver a cracking blow on Sally's skull — only to pull his punch, as it were, at the instant their heads collided. Having watched rams fighting, and heard their skulls smash into each other with a shocking detonation, I began to worry that our goatling might not survive this somewhat ferocious foreplay. But she stood her ground sturdily, *thock* after *thock* and was rewarded, almost as an afterthought, with an occasional swift coupling.

Since we had come so far at such a cost in petrol, it was important that one, at least, of these casual consummations did actually connect — especially as this was Sally's next-to-last chance of her current cycle. But Sovereign had been led forth by the woman of the house, who stood with us as we watched the goats. It reminded her, she said, of the time in her childhood when a bull was kept in the field beside the house "and the old men stood around all morning, smoking their pipes and talking and waiting to see would he perform."

A pipe might have given me something to chew on as I debated with myself: would it be proper to stoop down at the appropriate moment and look at exactly what was going on, or should I trust to appearances? City-bred decorum won out yet again, and it took a reassuring nod from my neighbour to make me satisfied that Sovereign had earned his £4.

The day had a coincidence in store. Having driven to Headford via Westport, we decided to return through the mountains by way of Cong, the Maam Valley and Leenane. Now that the early fog was dissipating, the peaks were tilting up to the sunshine through misty feather boas. The last of the bracken clung in swathes of raw sienna and those amazing winter willows of the west spun bright webs of orange twigs. All this gave Joyce Country a sharp-etched beauty the summer tourist never sees, for July and August, by comparison, are months drably lacking in magic.

There was quite a touch of magic in the sudden appearance ahead of us, on the road near Maam bridge, of a dozen large, shaggy, brown-and-white goats with horns like great curving broadswords. The last time I had met their equal was on a mountainside above the coast road north of Mulraney and I had taken those to be a remnant of native "wild" or feral stock. But these impressive creatures, roaming an agricultural valley and stripping bark from the wayside trees to the height of a man — were they wild or did they belong to someone? It made an excuse to stop at the Maam bridge pub.

The amiable, rheumy-eyed old man we drew into conversation named the owner of the goats and surmised that he probably kept them "to eat up any poison on the land — herbs and such things" (a variation on the folk belief, common to these islands, that running a billy goat with a herd of cows will prevent brucellosis). Goats, he thought, could be destructive creatures — they had eaten the oats in a field belonging to a neighbour "and then rolled about all over it, laughing and the dogs could do nothing."

At the same time, goats could be very brave. There was a goat had a kid up on the mountain and didn't a fox come along and try to seize the kid. "So she backed off along this ledge, with the kid pushed back between her legs, and the fox tried to rush her and didn't she hang him from her two horns, with his throat caught in the fork of them, until this man came along and killed him." He could show us the house of the man but hadn't he died since, God rest him.

He took a lift with us to the next pub up the valley. As he was getting into the car, Sally bleated from the boot but we said nothing. When we stopped to let him out, there was bleating again.

The old man paused and regarded us shrewdly. "Ye have a goat," he said.

"We do," we said, and in mischief added nothing more. We left him to conjecture how we might have come by a goat that day — and to make a good story of it, if he could.

Passing the Time

"AND WHAT DOES your husband do all day?" Even more wounding than the question, still sometimes asked of Ethna, has been her inability to answer it coherently. "You do so many things, it seems pointless to mention any one of them." And if she could summon up what might pass for a typical day, it would only partially persuade. If she were to say, for example that "He's putting up fences at the moment", they would think of all the days when I couldn't be putting up fences (being secretly convinced, very probably, that I do these things just once a week, for show).

What I am likely to be doing all day seems to become all the more hard to imagine in the depths of winter, when everyone in Connacht is popularly supposed to be hibernating. That I have to be a fulltime gardener for six months of the year seems just about credible, that the turf takes a month of days and the potato harvest can last for weeks can arouse some bewilderment. But that I don't have to *find* things to do in January and February seems, for some people, past all comprehension. Ethna sometimes asks them if they have ever done much camping, being ready to say that homesteading is a bit like that — being busy all day just surviving, improvising, doing what needs to be done. But usually they are not the camping kind.

The flux, the flow, the drifting balance of our days needs a particular kind of patience. Some occupations are better preparation for it than others, and journalism, fortunately, is a job that takes what comes. Those callings which live to the spirit of critical path analysis might introduce more order and efficiency to homesteading, but they could also lead one to break rather than bend. It is commonplace for me to step out of the door in the morning intending to do one specific task and then to come in for the lunchtime bowl of soup having done three or four entirely different jobs of maintenance or repair. This can, indeed, be frustrating, especially when I am pursuing some grand design, such as building another pillar of the turf shed or planting a fuchsia hedge. It does, I suppose, teach that life is a process of becoming.

But if what I do all day will never again be very predictable, our new life has at least begun to take on some shape and rhythm.

We are now entirely inured, for example, to starting the day at 5 a.m., when the loudest sound in the universe is the distant susurrus of surf along the strand. This has been one of our most important choices, forced on us originally by feeling simply too tired at the end of a summer day's work to do the creative things — writing, drawing or whatever — that we had promised ourselves. Now, even in the long darkness before a winter dawn, we are delighted to have exchanged a couple of jaded, passive evening hours for an equivalent period of alert, creative concentration (each at a separate window, wrapped in delicious silence, like Melleray monks). We may miss the best of television; we may have found the best of ourselves.

At about half-past seven, the first tentative bleats from The Hollow remind me that the goats are feeling hungry. While Ethna stokes the range and cooks breakfast, I clatter out with buckets of feed and the milk pail. With luck, I can have the milk strained and in the freezer before the weather forecast and the news.

After family breakfast (two eggs for me and half-a-dozen slices of wholemeal toast, heaped with cottage cheese), I carry on feeding the livestock in a routine refined in time and motion. Thus, when I take the goats their warm water, I retrieve the hay they have sniffed over and rejected and pass this on into the pony's manger. And when I go down the field, skidding in the mud, to let the hens out of their ark and give them their morning mash of barley and potato, I bring back a cabbage to chop for the goats. By ten o'clock, when I have put the goats out on their tethers and fed and released the ducks (who lay at around breakfast-time), the postman has pulled up at the gate in his yellow Mini.

We have been up for five hours, yet, thanks to half a lifetime's conditioning, we still feel that the day is ahead of us. From now until dusk, when I head into another round of feeding, milking and closing in the menagerie, the "real" work can be done.

In the original scenario of our new existence, I was to spend part of the day out painting. Among the equipment purchased for the move was a handsome Jullian box easel from France, with gleaming brass knobs and latches everywhere. Only last week, I was stocking it with tubes of colour, ready to make a serious, disciplined start at last — ten o'clock to one o'clock every day and let everything else go hang. I was going to paint Bridie's farmstead, in its grove of bare black sycamores. Then the lorry came with the timber.

So now I am fencing instead — building long, six-foot windbreaks across the field, clad with waste outer slabs of spruce from the Cornamona sawmill. The wood is fresh from the forest and smells as good as incense. I put up one stretch of fence in a gale and watched it stand to 50 mph gusts with scarcely a shiver. You can't go out painting in gales.

The Inheritors

IF IT WERE not for the BBC World Service, booming into our kitchen from the short waves, we might live out our pastoral lives all untroubled by the war in Chad, the mass resignation of the Sumatran cabinet or a host of other crises with which the RTE newsroom hesitates to bother us. Normally we overlook these lacunae in Montrose's foreign intelligence, but just occasionally we hear something from London that makes us wonder if Ireland is not being stranded, so to speak, on another wavelength from the rest of the Western world.

The other morning, for example, while I was watching Ethna making the cheese, there was a programme about preparations for nuclear war — preparations, that is, for surviving it. In China, it seems, no village is complete without its communal dugout, while the Swiss have tunnelled their mountains into Gruyere to provide shelter for 80% of the population, not to mention underground hospitals rather better than most countries keep on the surface.

In Britain, by contrast, the official line is fatalistic and only the regional governments have proper holes to go to. It has been left to private enterprise to develop a shelter industry and to set up survival condominiums like the underground refuge planned in Wiltshire: it will offer place to 10,000 people at £2,000 a time.

Ethna and I groaned in chorus — not at the inequity of having to buy one's survival, but at the thought of crawling out into the ruins in company with all those people clutching fur coats and briefcases. The people who would most want to survive a nuclear war are not necessarily the sort one would wish to know socially.

It may come as some surprise, indeed, that I do not see myself as the kind of noble inheritor chronicled in Olaf Stapledon's classic vision of *Last And First Men*. If one were looking at a map of Europe and given data on prevailing winds, ours is just the kind of corner one might pick as offering good prospects of a reasonably healthy survival. Remote from destruction and demoralising urban chaos, surely I would want to match my self-sufficient skills to the indomitable spirit of man? Should I not, at this moment, be digging a cave with a pick-axe somewhere up there on the ridge and preparing to stock it with a month's supply of tinned food and radio batteries?

I could well imagine myself doing this, perhaps, back in the 'fifties, when I was marching with the CND and singing "Och! Och! Get oot o' Holy Loch, for we dinna want Polaris!" (I happened to fall in with the Scottish contingent). I was well up in megadeaths in those days and needed no bidding from Dylan to "Rage, rage against the dying of the light!"

Now, I have not only lost my Irish Civil Defence handbook (which a macabre trick of memory insists was called *Bás In Eirinn*), but also the will to put up even a token struggle to survive World War Three. Despite our flight from the city and some of its refinements, I still find my purpose in a context of culture and civilisation. I would have no wish to outlive the destruction of Western society and watch the descent into a new Dark Age. Even if life could be resumed, here on this side of the hill, our sunsets lurid with the ashes of Europe and America, the sense of loss would be a sickness in itself.

Ethna, on the other hand, wouldn't mind surviving if she could do so in reasonable shape. The life instinct seems to burn more powerfully in women, and in this instance it reinforces curiosity, combativeness and a positive relish of problem solving. What, she demands, are we doing with books called *Living Off Nature* or a *History of Technology* in three volumes if we are never going to make our own candles or reinvent the loom?

Meanwhile (and may it be the longest meanwhile ever) she is, as I say, making cheese. Cottage cheese is simplicity itself, because unpasteurised milk goes wholesomely sour — unlike pasteurised milk, which rots — and once or twice a week it can be hung up in muslin for the whey to run out. Then it can be flavoured with chopped chives or garlic, or left with its own delicious tartness.

Hard cheese is another matter, needing knowledge and equipment and a good cook's attention to timing. It also takes a gallon of milk for every pound of cheese, so that, at this time of year, we must hoard milk day by day in the freezer and make, say five pounds of cheese once a month.

This is when Ethna brings out her galvanised buckets, big thermometer, and the cheese-press and moulds she had made about 20 years ago when she tried to set up cheese-making as a cottage industry in Killala. She designed the moulds to produce a distinctively shaped cheese — triangular, with rounded corners — and it looks most professional on the table. Before she got the press, she made her cheese in ordinary round moulds (fabricated in blocked tins by tinkers out on the bog) and used rocks off the ditch as weights.

Exact temperatures and timings are the heart of cheesecraft, plus a steady hand with the knife. When the rennet separates the milk into curd and whey, the curd — like a soft blancmange — has to be sliced into tiny cubes about half an inch square. Then begins the process of draining and pressing which, together with temperatures, varies in its details from one kind of cheese to another.

We are making the "crofter" cheese (which the Department of Agriculture, in its excellent how-to-do-it Leaflet 72, called, confusingly, "cottage" cheese). This is a semi-hard cheese of mild flavour, not unlike a dryish white Cheddar, which matures in about four weeks. With Nancy's low, mid-winter return on feeding, we reckon it is costing about £1 a pound; in late spring, when her milk yield has risen, the cost could be half that. Valued at the 45p a pint paid for goat's milk in the cities, our cheese would be worth £3.60 a pound, which puts it in the epicurean class.

Making cheese from frozen milk, rather than from a mix of fresh evening and morning milk, means that the cream is lost in the whey. But we capture the "goodness" of it, so to speak, in a substance very few people in Ireland can have tasted — Norwegian whey cheese. When the whey is evaporated by being left to simmer on top of the range for a day or two, it sets finally into a golden substance closely resembling peanut butter and tasting like a blend of Camembert, Marmite and condensed milk. It can be used as a spread, and a little of it goes a long way. Boiled too long, indeed, it resembles dark brown toffee and, as one of our books observes, "can only be eaten in saltspoonsful by the very brave."

Norwegian whey cheese is highly nutritious and just the thing, perhaps, for the food cupboard in your fall-out shelter.

Beastly Chores

CITY FASTIDIOUSNESS IS slow to fade. When I walk through mud, my toes still curl involuntarily inside my Wellingtons: I find myself trying to tiptoe instead of squelching stolidly on. But in the matter of rural smells I am less squeamish. My nostrils, now quite recovered from all those years of chain-smoking and freshly-sensitised by the cleanest air in Ireland, can tell if somebody is feeding silage, or has dipped his sheep, half a dozen fields away. Yet there are very few smells in the countryside which seem to me unpleasant; perhaps it is all in the mind.

Even the different dungs I have to deal with are far from uniformly foul. Mucking out the pony, for example, can be positively enjoyable: his droppings seem merely to condense the more fragrant fractions of his hay. Ethna, certainly, would rather do this than change a nappy (what a sexist observation!). And as for the goats' pellets, they are quite as innocuous as those of sheep or rabbits — shining brown raisins of dung without much local smell at all.

Cowdung, the omnipresent "muck" of farming, seems to vary a lot in olfactory impact according to diet and vintage. the dark green smell of an early summer cowpat, plopping down into a verdant meadow, can catch the throat like whiskey fumes, whereas the muck that I spread in the spring for the potatoes comes from a drier winter diet; its smell seems to cling to my clothing like the cloying, sweet fermentation of the silage that nourished it. Only in the forking out of muck from the pile behind a neighbour's byre, a pile beginning to seethe with bubbles of methane and ammonia, can cowdung actually wring a gasp from me.

It is when we move from animal droppings to those of birds that we begin to near intolerable effluvia. I have heard of ornithologists who, landing on ocean rocks to study the breeding of seabird colonies, have come near to swooning, if not actual suffocation, from the gas of the deposited guano. How men were persuaded to dig it up for the fertiliser industry, I canot imagine.

Henshit, owing more to barley and potatoes than worms and beetles, is marginally less noxious than the fishy distillations of gannets and guillemots. It would possibly be even less offensive if I could bring myself to clear the dropping board of the night ark once a week rather than once a month. And it was sheer length of accumulation, certainly, which helped to make excavation of the ducks' quarters this week the most noisome ordeal of my country career.

The shed in The Hollow, beside the stream, was built for ducks and geese. I housed the birds on raised wire-netting frames so that their droppings would fall to the floor for periodic removal. There was a big clean-up when we stopped keeping geese (because they needed grass we didn't have). There was another after the big flood that silted up the shed with sand. There was another when we got the goats and installed them in two-thirds of the shed: the ducks were left in residence at one end.

Goats don't need mucking out very often unless one is selling milk to the public and has to be frightfully hygienic. They will be very comfortable on the hot-bed system — allowing their litter to accumulate, liberally laced with droppings, until they have a magnificent compost heap of spoiled hay, rushes, bracken and old cabbage leaves which heats up under the goats and raises the temperature nicely for milking on winter mornings. It needs to be cleared only once or twice a year. By last month, our goats' bed was a solid, cosy mattress 18 inches thick. The ducks' loo next door, meanwhile, was a sort of sealed-off mudflat, deepening imperceptibly day by day and giving no reminder of its presence so long as it was not disturbed.

This month, however, it became apparent that young Sally's visit to the puck had achieved its purpose and that she would be kidding in June. In a sudden fit of solicitude, I decided the goats must have the whole shed, with proper raised wooden shelves to sleep on, and that the ducks must be evicted to a new house of their own. I built this next day, from forestry slabs and old asbestos roofing.

Only the dedicated compost gardener will appreciate fully the zest with which I then knocked together a special bin, several cubic yards in capacity, to receive the goats' bed and duckshit in alternate layers. It would all rot down to a humus of unsurpassed richness, a positive Escoffier among composts.

Few stomachs anywhere, I venture to claim, could have held so firm while spooning up with a road-mender's shovel the black, glutinous mud beneath the ducks' netting — mud as vile as any that has oozed around the Liffey's pilings. Our ducks may have eaten every slug and snail from our acre, and for that I have to be grateful, but as I scraped the last corner clean and hosed the floor down with Dettol, I felt I had known what it was to be a latrine orderly.

And while we are considering the less-than-idyllic aspects of the homesteading life, the pony has now been sponged from end to end with Tixol to deal with his mange. He didn't like the process, but reared up out of my grip only when Ethna's sponging approached his more delicate parts ("Perhaps he wouldn't mind so much," she said in all earnestness, "if you did those bits," whereupon we both burst into laughter).

Now, on vet's advice, we have to douse the two goats as well. This sort of war on parasites — lice, ticks and myriad mites — will now, it seems, be a regular part of our lives. One neighbouring family routinely dips or sponges every animal on the farm each spring, — not just the sheep and cattle, but the pony, dogs and cats.

Our small cat, Sooty, limped home the other morning with a shockingly mangled forepaw. It seemed to have been crushed and bitten right through and was swollen to three times its size. We could only speculate on her opponent — rat, stoat, badger? — or wonder about gin traps.

Apart from readmitting her to the warmth of the kitchen range, we left her alone to lick her wound. The paw wept fluid for days but gradually began to subside. She still cannot put it to the ground, but gets around remarkably well. One balmy day this week, I found her lying on the ditch in the sun, apparently convalescing. But then she showed me the rat holes she had found, and thrust her injured paw and half her body into one, her tail twitching angrily from side to side.

A Bit of a Breeze

ON ONE OF HIS winter visits to the mainland, our friend Gustin from Inishbofin stopped off for a drink in Louisburgh and met a man he knew, a fellow-fisherman from Clare Island. The wind was getting up from the south and they fell into an amiable argument about extremes of weather. The man from Clare Island was claiming that a low-lying island like Inishbofin couldn't know what a proper gale was. Really to feel the wind, he insisted, you must live on an island that has a mountain: it made all the difference. Gustin was amused and indignant. To argue about gales with a Bofin man!

He stayed the night with us, bedding down on the sofa in the living room, by the fire. He might have a noisy night, we apologised: the wind was always worse from Mweelrea. In the morning, we found him hollow-eyed and chastened: he hadn't slept at all. The Clare Island man was right, he said and a mountain did make a difference.

As I write, the wind from Mweelrea — a south-easterly gale with storm-force gusts — has been blowing for forty-eight hours without a pause, the longest gale from that quarter in more than a year. The mountain itself is hiding in a dark, dense haze, and the ridge of Six Noggins above us seems to crouch lower than usual in the landscape, as if seeking a firmer hold.

We have learned by now not to look for sympathy in the radio weather reports, or even much acknowledgement of our trial by wind. "Belmullet hazy and four degrees", chirruped Valerie McGovern this morning — not a word of the townlands being lifted off the face of the earth. The Meteorological Office, obsessed with whether or not the sun will shine, lists a gale warning almost as an afterthought: there is Ireland's weather and there are separate gales for fishermen. A Mayo county councillor was complaining the other day that the Met. Office gives the West a bad name as the place that rain is always spreading from, but what I object to is being told that the day will be "windy" in tones that suggest that we should all head off to Salthill for a bracing stroll along the prom.

"Breezy" is the word preferred on this side of the hill — a wilful understatement that used to exasperate me until I came to understand its significance. It is a propitiation, an attempt at sympathetic magic. If we all shout out "Breezy day!" as we cling to our bushes and boulders, breezy it may magically become. The greeting "Soft day!" as rain falls torrentially was devised to a similar formula.

So it may be my insistence on calling a gale a gale that brings down the wrath of the mountain in great lumps of wind aimed peculiarly and privately at the Viney homestead. The Met. Office, in describing gales from the Atlantic, may warn of "severe gusts in exposed places", but it seems to know nothing about these maleficent juggernauts gathered in from the plains of Galway, raced up the Maam Valley, whipped round the bend of Killary and sent swerving over the shoulder of Mweelrea to thunder down on our acre.

My network of new fences — "windbreaks", as I had the nerve to call them — make a gleaming target, visible for miles. One of them was built specifically to shield the Brussels sprouts from the mountain gusts; a palisade of vertical, six-foot forestry slabs spaced to let the wind through, properly calmed down, but not the hens.

But the fence that faces south-east must also face north-west. We get gales from both directions — so on which side should I nail the slabs? I gambled wrongly, as it happened, and saw the slabs plucked off within a week by a gale from the north-west. I hammered them back with longer nails and braced the fence with props on the south-east side.

Yesterday morning, peering out into the howling dawn, I saw that yes, of course, I should have added props on the north-west side as well. I staggered down the field with stout spars, a steel mallet and a pocket full of five-inch nails. Heaving the fence upright with my shoulders, I blinked away the wind-tears and tried not to hit my thumb.

This morning I was almost afraid to look out of the window. The fences were still shuddering in the unceasing barrage. Some of them have a drunken tilt here and there and a few more slabs have been peeled away like strips of cardboard, But the fences stand, they stand!

In such a gale as this, we feel enveloped by the wind. It flows around the house like a great torrent around a stone, sucking and pressing and searching. We shut dampers down tightly on the kitchen range and the living-room stove, but still the fire is snatched up the chimney by the rush of air above, the heat dispelled by a thousand surreptitious draughts. We battle out to the turf stack to fill yet another bag and find the stack's plastic covering shredded into fluttering black pennants. The turf dust whirls up into our eyes and lodges, scratchy, blinding with more tears.

The wind makes difficulties everywhere. Bringing armfuls of hay from the shed, I have somehow to keep a grip on the door to stop it smashing back off its hinges or chopping off my fingers. Down in the hen run, where the birds are bowled in a heap against the fence, I fight to tie down the lids of the nesting boxes while keeping hold of half-dozen-eggs. Up on the flat roof of the house extension, I try to fasten down the cable of the television aerial that has been scraping and slapping since the gale began. Eventually, I climb the ladder with a concrete block and pin the cable with it like a boulder on a snake.

Accustomed to wind as we have become, a gale like this begins to wear at our composure, so that each new express train of a gust makes us tense in sympathy with the straining rafters of the flat roof, the shuddering slates of the old house. Is this to be the time when something gives?

The Long View

PERCHED ON THE roof of the new garden shed, daubing the raw white rafters with creosote, I took time to track a shaft of sun across the foothills of the mountain. It was lighting up the fields in patches of intense lettuce-green in the smoky, blue-grey shadow, and I found myself trying to calculate the particular mix of paint that would pin that glowing green to a canvas. Then the reek of the creosote reminded me what the brush in my hand was for.

This is the fourth spring of my procrastination. Much more of it and my precious store of oil paints will start to wither in their tubes: cobalts and cadmiums losing their sap, their vigour. Hair will fall from my brushes; my canvases will wrinkle up.

Four springs? Thirty springs, more like it. It is quite that long since solemn teachers, guiding grammar school careers, urged me to persevere with painting — in order to teach it. Journalism? Too uncertain, too precarious! Just what a teenager waited to hear.

So the painter took a back seat, still untutored, experimenting now and then in bachelor garrets, disdaining the results. Journalism leaves no room for parallel vocations. Real painters take jobs as postmen, night telephonists, dishwashers, and keep their eyes and minds for themselves. I spent lunchtimes in art galleries, hung around real painters, let them tell me to stick with what I was good at.

There was, of course, the sabbatical winter in Connemara — Viney's grey period, twenty years ago. One or two passable paintings survived, hostages to one of these days. Marooning myself on islands produced one or two more. They hinted at what might happen if only I got *down* to it. . .So, making time for painting became one good reason for our defection from Dublin and the regular, salaried life. Once my day was my own, it could be shared between the hoe and the paintbrush.

But where procrastination is a habit, the homesteading life offers all manner of excuses. There are always other, more urgent priorities of food and fuel and shelter. "Getting settled in" can take years. And until we build the porch, with a studio for me at one end, I simply have "nowhere" to paint — nowhere, that is, except the immense, overpowering landscape outside the door.

For some time I would argue that this particular corner of Mayo is virtually unpaintable. Its vistas are so enormous that one would need a canvas the size of a Cinemascope screen. There isn't a decent vertical in sight unless one includes a whole mountain or piles up the clouds like Paul Henry. These vast horizontal sweeps of sand and sea and treeless hillside give the eye no pause or shelter.

But then I accompanied a real painter, Derek Hill, on an expedition to Inishkea, the island off the Mullet, and watched him do battle with landscapes of barest essentials — a glimmering line of sand between sea and sky, a single cloud rising from a round, dull hill — and capture immensities of light and distance on the backs of cigar-box lids eight inches by six.

Weather and time of year could be used for more delay. Nobody, short of Van Gogh, could expect me to set up in a wind this strong, even with a rock to hold the easel down. And whole months can be written off for their unpainterly pallor: who would want to paint the dead, dusty greens of July and August, when he has the palette of November blazing in his mind; the cobalt lakes, the gold and crimson grasses of the bog, the smouldering siennas of dead fern? But the days in November, again, are so short.

And is it not too late, in any case, to be painting this sort of landscape in the age of the colour Instamatic? Is there any point in rehashing Henry or mulling over Millet and ending up, if one works at it, in the window of Combridges? That way lie sunsets and rainbows, cliches of mere physics that Ethna and I waste our exclamations upon.

So, with all the plausible reasons for not getting down to it, and the spring sowing season pressing its demands, why do my thoughts keep wandering off to a little niche in the landscape about three miles from here? It is not easy to reach with easel and canvas: how, with my talent for difficulties, could it be! I have to go to where the road ends, at the very foot of the mountain, and set off across a deep, empty strand to the headland beyond — this, of course, attainable only at certain stages of the tide. Beyond the headland is another white and flawless strand that stretches to the corner of the Killary, to a spit of rock where Paul Henry, indeed, once perched his easel to look back along the awesome avenue of the fiord.

Halfway along this hidden strand, I turn aside to a cleft in the mountain side to a place the old steel-engraved Admiralty map calls "Mulgarve". We take this as a rendering of *maol-garbh* "bare and rough" — a name for a village that must have seemed to the navy men of 1848 like a place at the end of the world.

It is a rough place, certainly, with great boulders and outcrops so mingled with the tumbled ruins that it is hard to sort out man's work from nature's. But what draws me to it is the fact that it is *not* bare. By contrast with the mountain slope that rises sheer behind it, its growth is an almost exotic tangle of native holly trees, ivy and thorn, all crowding in around a splashing waterfall. At the foot of the glen are old buildings still used as an outfarm, and this is where the sheep are penned for dipping and shearing.

All the vegetation is very strange and special. The holly trees are twisted wraiths, stretched out on the wind like figures in a Jack Yeats painting, branches bare and white as old bones. The ivy crouches to the rocks, stems hugely corded from the years of clinging, plant and rock interfolding in towering bas reliefs. And the thorn bushes are individual sculptures — spiky, trembling, totemistic.

There are a thousand paintings in the cleft of *maol-garbh*. I may get down to it, at last.

The Swing of It

IF YOU DON'T get your turf off the mountain by Bonfire Night, June 24th, you won't get it off at all, or so the local saying goes. That's a little dogmatic, like most wisdom of its kind, but its urgency does have point. Mweelrea can be most unforgiving to the dilatory turf cutter. A spatter of a shower here below can be a grey curtain of rain across the darkened flank of the mountain, and a wet July and August can reconstitute the bog into jelly.

Last year, I made the mistake of hoping that the spring drought could mean a fine summer and misspent its brassy, scouring days, so perfect for the bog, at other work. Those who seized the weather and went cutting early found a kind of magic worked on the turf: "It would dry in spite of you," said my neighbour. Sods were gathered where they had fallen from the *sleán*. We, on the other hand, found ourselves struggling through the midges at autumn, retrieving wet turf in half-loads so as not to sink the tractor.

"Never again!" I vowed. And when the drought arrived again last month I scrambled to catch up, to get manure spread and potatoes sown, and not to be the last poor fool on the bog. By Easter Sunday, when the brilliance of the day proclaimed — as clearly as if a bell had been rung — the townland migration, we took our place in the procession of families as if moved by some suitably timeless impulse.

There are few situations in Connacht's rural life in which one's industry and aptitude are so immediately on view as on the bog, which sets them out in silhouette along the bank as in an Egyptian frieze. Much as I regret, for sociable reasons, our isolation across the river from the main concourse of the bog, at least we keep our small disgraces more or less to ourselves. The footings of turf left over from last year, which should have been lumped months ago, could be carried away discreetly. And, as much to the point, I could ease myself into the work this past week without feeling watched — or not too closely — if I stopped to straighten my back.

For though my hands are now calloused and my neck as red as brick, I can still get aches and pains no less grievous than in my spasms of gardening in suburban Dublin.

One reason for changing lives at 45 was my feeling that this was quite late enough to be building a durable physique; at 50 or 55, the clay would be starting to crumble. I am sure now that this was right. It is not any one task that tests the homesteader, but exertion that gives no respite, no mending time, right from the very first day. After almost four years, I am lifting and heaving and hauling as much as ever.

That I still get pains in my back is disappointing but hardly surprising. It was quite early on, after all, that I dislocated a thumb without knowing it and had to find a chiropractor, in Limerick, to snap it back into place. While he was at it, he untangled a few cords of muscle in my back and arms in a way that made me aware, really for the first time, of the *mechanical* intricacy of the body. One reads so much about its chemistry, its cells and nerves, that the marvels of its ordinary wires and pulleys get overlooked. In the lethargy of city life, muscle and sinew lie slack beneath the fat, but here one begins to wonder at the way things work — at, for example, the hand's ability to retain a heavy bag slung over the shoulder by the pressure of one finger.

Of course, the muscles must often be strained out of alignment. When I visit Michael, down the boreen, at the end of a day's digging or stooping over seed beds, and a little groan escapes me as I sit down, he gives a friendly chortle of recognition. In this corner of the world, back ache is part of the natural human condition once in middle age. And yet, much of what the farmers (and so many others) accept as inevitable, or blame on rheumatism or arthritis, must be no more than the simple, muscular strains or maladjustments that football trainers see every day. What a pity that most doctors cannot be bothered with the manipulative and massaging skills of the chiropractor or osteopath, or even the experienced sports coach.

As a labour designed to seek out the sensitive muscle, cutting turf can have few equals. The most severe work comes right at the start, first in the undercutting and lifting of the surface scraw and then in throwing out the sods of the top spit to leave room for those to come. Even with the swing of the *sléan* to help, lobbing a sod weighing half a stone a distance of eight or nine yards and doing that several hundred times in a row can be quite punishing to the torso. And, for all my fitness, the first day of cutting this spring left me as sore as if I had been kicked in the ribs by a horse.

This happened partly because of an innocent question from Ethna. "Why," she wanted to know, "are you throwing them all in the same place?" She indicated the mounting pile of fresh sods, each one of which, ideally, should be occupying a separate, dry space on the bank.

I explained that the mound was not deliberate, but resulted from my new determination not to look to see where the sods were landing. "Just watch Michael Mac over there," I enjoined "Does he turn his head to look? He does not. It would break his rhythm. It's time I got rhythm too."

We both paused to watch Michael Mac cut turf. He made it seem effortless. Almost before one sod had landed, another was flying from his *sléan*. There were no piles of sods, no glutinous black wodges to be prised apart. His sods lay like chocolates on a tray. "And he does it without looking", I insisted. "Nobody looks except me".

"He does it without breaking them, too." said Ethna gently, regarding the fragments at her feet. "But then, he gets more practice." That, certainly, was true. By the start of June last year, Michael had seven trailer loads dry and home. Then, to be on the safe side, he went on to cut three or four more.

I resumed the quest for rhythm, but now so conscious of every sod that flew apart on landing, or smacked into one already there, that all continuity of motion was lost. I tried looking and not looking, lobbing high and pitching low, throwing over my shoulder or straight ahead, but still they broke or smacked together. I ended with a ragged fringe of half-sods and this ache in the solar plexus. I retrieved what pride I could from tossing out the deeper spits intact and from retrieving the last buttery morsels from among the bright bones of the bog deal.

Time and Tide

"AND OF COURSE," said a visitor last week, gazing from the doorstep down to the strand and the islands, "you must get lovely fresh fish all the time." We forebore to say that the last fish from the freezer, months ago, was a sad little haddock bought from the itinerant van that sometimes wends its way from Killala. We are amost embarrassed to talk of self-sufficiency and yet to take so little from the sea.

It is true that last month, which still had an "r" in it, we processed two hundred-weights of mussels, steaming them open in saucepans on the range and then scooping the meat from the shells into cartons for the freezer. The job took most of two days, and by the time we had sealed the twentieth pound, we felt we never wished to see another mussel.

But these had not been harvested from our corner of the coast: they came from the sheltered reaches of the Killary, eighteen miles away through the mountains. In the gentle waters of Bundorragha, a mussel can loll about in the shallows and wax fat on plankton, just as one can leave a currach there, moored at the end of a line for weeks together. But here, on the open shore outside the mountains, a mussel grows no bigger than a thumbnail and it lashes itself tightly to the rock with silken threads. Our currach, too, must be tied down in its cranny above the waves.

We wait to see if this summer will lend any more sense to maintaining a boat that so rarely goes to sea: whether, between winch and trolley, we can solve the problem of launching and retrieving her without anyone else's help; whether there may, after all, be enough fine, calm days to spare for setting and lifting the trammel.

We began with such high hopes. Half-a-dozen good hauls between June and September would fill the freezer with fish for the winter: surely we could manage that! But we reckoned without the simple logistics of managing a currach that was built for two strong men, on a coast so bare of shelter that the nearest berth for a boat is a niche in the rocks a mile from the nearest road.

We also had to learn some of the realities of our neighbours' lives

— realities we now find mirrored in our own. The work of summer is hard and long, and rest, when it comes, is wanted. No one has leisure which needs occupying or energy to dissipate in physical recreation. There is no impulse to go "messing about in boats" as any sort of social activity. Handling a currach is too strenuous to be undertaken in any but a serious and gainful way. Fishing may be pleasurable but it is not a relaxation (nor should it be, perhaps, on a coast as perilous as this one) and a man who gives time to it expects a return from the catch).

When this outlook is matched to the competing priorities for every fine day of the summer — bog, hay or silage — our hopes of recruiting our neighbours to fishing expeditions can be seen as altogether too sanguine. Those who fish seriously have preferred, understandably, to go after their own catches, not share in ours; those who might fish now and again have found little time for it these past three drenching summers. Either we find ways of fishing on our own, or we put the currach up for sale.

Meanwhile, there is fishing to be done off the rocks, mainly for pollack and mackerel. Pollack is the beautifully streamlined, golden-olive fish that haunts the underwater reefs. Even a two- or three-pound fish will put up a stirring fight, and hooking one of the bigger ones that sometimes wander inshore can be very exciting indeed. Pollack is not outstandingly good to eat — like a somewhat watery cod — but it does make fine fishcakes.

Until you know your ground, standing on the same rocky ledge time after time and casting at all stages of the tide, pollack fishing can be costly, as one bait after another hooks into rock or weed and you haul despairingly on the line until it snaps. My favourite bait for spinning is the "German Sprat," a slender, slightly dished, silver spoon. At least a dozen of these must now be glinting along the weedy depths between here and the Killary. It would be cheaper to make up my own rubber eels, or to go hunting live ones with a table fork under stones in the channel through the strand.

The best time to fish for pollack — the "suicide hour," as the Cornish anglers call it — is the last hour of light at evening or the first at dawn, when pollack rise up in the water to feed and one can spin near the surface without fear of losing tackle. But it would need quite special determination to try this at either of the best pollack stations on our stretch of coast, since each demands a lengthy hike along the shore and perhaps some anxious wading through the tide.

My favourite fishing place is a steep-walled, grass-topped islet called Dooneen, at the entrance to Killary Harbour. At one side is the exquisite strand at the foot of Mweelrea Mountain; at the other, the clear, chill water of the fiord, deepening swiftly to twenty fathoms. To cast out into their shadows is to invite the fierce unknown, even if it always comes up as pollack.

At this time of the year, Dooneen is inhabited each day by two brawny fellows from Connemara, on the other side of the fiord. For weeks on end they sprawl among the sea pinks, caps pulled down against the glare from the water, keeping watch on the long salmon net that reaches out from the point of the islet like a great gate left ajar. They are not unfriendly, but one senses that they would rather not have anyone bobbing about on the skyline and making splashes every other minute.

For our first expedition of the season (Ethna and I go off fishing together as other couples go golfing), we went to the second-best station, a rocky promontory close to where we keep the currach. I confess at once that we caught nothing, casting out into the top of a spring tide from rocks made black and greasy by the evening drizzle. And as we came back over the high ground above the dunes, we could see that the tide had run up behind them, into the lake, and this great meander gleaming in the dusk would bar the way home for an hour or two more.

There are some contortions of landscape that have to be walked to be understood and we have never yet made full sense of the land beyond the lakes, with its cliffs and marshes and sandy combes. Now, in the drizzly gloaming, we discovered that the way around the big lake, though a long and stumbling detour, is not as difficult as it looks. One does not, after all, come to a gurgling end among the reeds or have to climb the ivy up an overhang. Instead, right at the marshy roots of the lake, we came upon a path of stone flags, winding through the wetland for a hundred yards or more. So rare is a footpath in this rough-and-ready landscape that it seemed more like a fairy gift than the product of a farmer's hard work.

Under the Hedge

ON A MOIST and gloomy evening, with ragged wreaths of mist hanging low around the mountain, Ethna went out to The Hollow to shut in the ducks. She returned bearing a large wholly white mushroom she had found gleaming in the dusk. Its sudden appearance in the crepuscular drizzle, pushing up through the old nest of hay where the goose used to lay her eggs, struck her as spooky, but in a manner of science fiction rather than witchcraft. The mushroom was so sculpturally perfect, so archetypically exotic, so newly arrived. It would certainly be worth drawing. Might it also be worth eating?

That demanded a name for it. After half-an-hour with our mushroom books, we thought we were sure what it was. Groping through the key of the "Collins Guide to Mushrooms and Toadstools" and scrutinising scores of colour photographs and minutely detailed descriptions in "The Encyclopedia of Mushrooms" we were virtually certain that what we had was the Grisette, *Amanita vaginata,* in a white variety found in mountainous regions. If we were right, then its flesh would be "exquisite" promised the Encyclopedia, superior even to the field mushroom *Agaricus campestris.*

But what if we were wrong? Beside it on the page were other members of the *Amanita* family, each growing up from the remnants of its veil. And there was the Death Cap, *Amanita phallodes,* the most poisonous fungus known to man. "In many ways," said the Encyclopedia of our Grisette, "the species resembles the deadly poisonous *Amanita phallodes,* the only marked difference being its lack of a ring."

Well, we would *see* that our mushroom hadn't a ring, couldn't we, and ours had this whitish-grey cap, not a yellow-brown one like the Death Cap in the book. On the other hand, the Grisette in the encyclopedia's photograph had an ashy-brown cap — the white variety was only mentioned in the text — and the painting of it in the Collins Guide, even at half-size, seemed altogether too small. Our eyes slid across to *Amanita virosa,* the Destroying Angel, a wholly white toadstool quite as deadly as the Death Cap, but rarer. There were differences, again, but still...was it worth it, for a few, perhaps "exquisite", mouthfuls?

It was the classic dilemma of the novice fungus hunger — being almost totally certain, not wanting to be put off one's judgement by irrational fears, and yet not wanting either to blunder into a slow and horrible death. The white *Amanitas,* and the Death Cap in particular, cause at least 90% of all fatal fungal poisionings. We decided to play safe.

Next morning, however, we were able to retrieve our confidence as amateur fungus fanciers. If the Grisette could be lured forth by the unseasonably humid weather, perhaps there were other species to find. I followed the stream up the hillside to the grassy hollows where autumn field mushrooms have sprung up in the past. There were furls of white sheep's wool to fool me from a distance — but no mushrooms. The only toadstools I could see were the little yellow parasols in the cow-pats in Bridie's meadow.

It was Ethna again, rummaging in the shadows under the old fuchsia hedge, who made the find — a cluster of big, fleshy mushrooms with wavy, cream-coloured caps, white gills and stout, curved stems. The books identified them readily as Saint George's Mushroom, known in France as the Spring Mushroom and eaten enthusiastically in China (where else!). It tastes and smells strongly of newly-ground meal.

By all the rules, St George's Mushroom should not be growing on our acre at all: it belongs much more typically on chalky grassland. But scattered through the leafmould under the hedge are lumps of old mortar rubble, and the lime from this must have turned the balance of our normally acid soil.

The mushrooms gave us a delicious dinner (sautéed gently, then simmered in our own parsley wine), with enough left over to freeze. It was our most successful introduction to a new species since we gathered a basketful of Shaggy Ink Caps from the playing fields of King's Hospital school in suburban Dublin (they have tall, white caps with curly scales, hence their other name Lawyers' Wigs).

Some readers will find this whole line of conduct somewhat peculiar, knowing mushrooms only as little pink-lined buttons, trapped under plastic in trays on the supermarket shelf. The Irish share with the British a suspicion of wild fungi as a source of food which amounts almost to mycophobia. The French, the Italians, the Poles eat a wide variety of mushrooms and toadstools (the distinction has little useful meaning), but although there are about forty species worth eating in these islands, the only wild fungus to be much sought after is the common field mushroom.

Even Cyril and Kit O'Ceirin, in their excellent book, "Wild and Free", do not venture beyond the field mushroom and how to cook, pickle or dry it. They recall the great mushroom autumn of 1976, when they filled two four-stone bags from a five-acre field and left as many after them. We, too, remember that year, when the mushrooms were growing on the hillside right from the mountain fence to the very edge of the sea. Many were the Horse Mushroom, *Agaricus arvensis,* with caps as big as tea plates and every bit as edible and good as their smaller relations. Weight for weight, mushrooms hold more protein than potatoes or cabbage and are rich in a number of the B vitamins.

It seems unlikely that our sparsely-nourished hillside will offer us much of a choice of fungi; the St George's Mushrooms are a most untypical bonus. When the mushrooms return — they need a good summer before they autumn showers — there will also be puffballs to cook in slices, though nothing as meatily spectacular as the Giant Puffball, big as a football, which I found at a Wicklow roadside last September. The conifer forestry over the hill may have a few edible species, and the deciduous woods of Delphi in the Doolough Valley are dank as any rain forest and may hold all kinds of surprises.

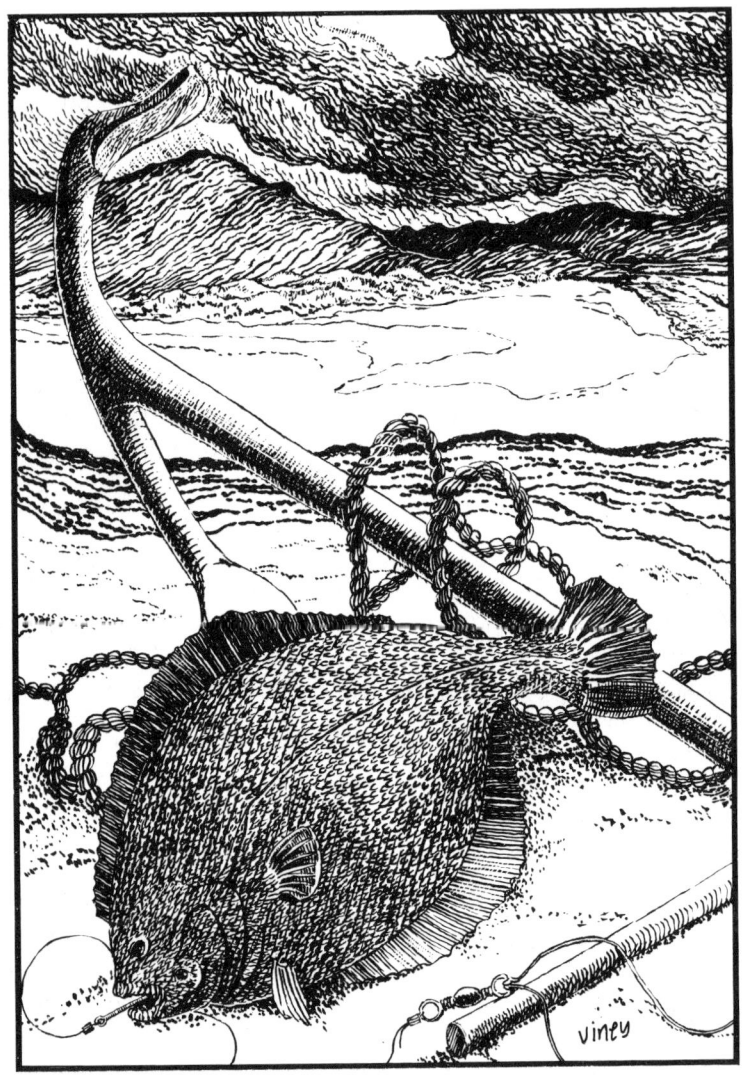

Nightline

AMONG THE EQUIPMENT we brought to the self-sufficient side of this new life was a present from a fisherman friend: a long-line, or spillet, of a hundred hooks, to be set in the deeps from our currach. It had taken time and skill to put together and looked most efficient, the hooks lined up safely in a slot cut into an oaken board, and the long loops of line taped together in a hank to stop them getting tangled.

Until last week, however, the long-line had never got wet. Because of our difficulties in using the currach, we have scarcely begun to use the trammel net properly, let alone learn the art of the spillet. Every time I opened the box where we kept it, and thought of the care that had gone into making it, I would feel guilty.

From time to time we could consider setting the line, not from the currach, but from the shore. The idea bobbed up again this week when we were talking to the fishing tackle dealer in Louisburgh. He reminded us that the plaice should be coming into the strand below us: had we ever thought of setting a spillet?

One problem holding us back was lack of bait. Lugworms would be the ideal, but our corner of coast is scoured so fiercely by the tides and pounded so hard by the surf that it is no place for worms to live. To dig lug, we would have to go north to Clew Bay, where the sands are more sheltered and stable and richer in food. And to us, £2 worth of petrol is a lot to gamble on one or two settings of a spillet.

Mussels would be another prime bait, but these, too, are far away up the Killary. We still had some in the freezer, and they might just work, even parboiled. But, by coincidence that seemed an omen, there arrived at the gate the fish van from North Mayo with its last few boxes of mackerel, welcome both to eat and as bait.

For the experienced long-line fisherman, the readying and baiting of so short a length as a hundred hooks would be a brief and brisk operation. His hand has dexterity for hooks, his eye knows the quickest way through a tangle. The hooks on a long-line occur at about six-foot intervals. Each is joined to the line by a two-foot nylon trace and a swivel. Given the snarls that an angler using only one hook can get into, the potential of a spillet in our amateur hands should be obvious. When I began, I did not even know enough to hang the hook-board on the wall so that the loops of line could be shaken gently free of each other. You do not try to unravel them on a table.

We did know that we should ready the line by coiling it down into a big, round basket and sticking or hanging the baited hooks around the edge in sequence. We did not have such a basket and hoped that a plastic washing-up basin would do. We discovered too late that a shallow, slippery container lets the hooks spring off the rim over the side and twine together.

Our mistake had us kneeling on the sand at the edge of the ebb tide at half-past ten at night, peering at a hopeless snarl of line enmeshing the last thirty hooks of the spillet. Neither of us had brought our spectacles, and even if we had, the rain spitting down from the indigo mountain would have rendered them useless. We would have to let the tangle stay.

The line was stretched along the sand between two small dinghy anchors. To be on the safe side, a rope linked one of the anchors to a barnacled rib of the old wooden wreck, revealed when the tide recedes. Each of the baits was covered with a handful of sand — "otherwise", warned one of our fishing books, "there will be a gull or two to deal with".

The appearance of the wreck's black ribs as the tide ebbed again next morning sent us hurrying down the boreen, past the squealing lapwings and across the half-mile of sand to the sea. The line was just emerging from the waves, many of its hooks festooned with seaweed. But yes, there was just one fish, a fine, plump flounder. The last time I ate flounder was in New Orleans, and to me it seemed a fair exchange for two monotonous mackerel. No fish, and we might have been cast down; one fish, and anything was possible.

For our second attempt, we used just half the line, ranging the hooks around the narrow rim of a bucket and waiting to bait them until the line was safely stretched between the anchors. We set it at midday and by teatime were looking down to a spring tide flooding in across the sand to the very edge of the *duach*.

The evening turned foul, with a stiff southerly wind and heavy rain. The trouble with any sort of trap, be it a rabbit snare or a baited hook, is that it has to be revisited, whatever the weather. As we trudged out over the strand in the gathering dusk, it was hard to tell the boundaries of sand, sea and sky: all were merging in tones of silvery grey, smudged together by wind and water.

The baits were gone, but we had no fish. We felt sharply disappointed. Were it not for our solitary flounder, we might have felt we were wasting our time. But then, towards the end of the line, appeared a still, bedraggled shape that betrayed what had happened. It was a young herring gull, hooked through the cheek and drowned. A handful of sand may hide a bait for long enough at dusk, but in bright day, as the first wave swirls over it, sand is obviously no camouflage against the hovering gulls. Perhaps I shall have to wade out with the spillet into an incoming tide.

By the time we had retrieved the line, keeping our backs to the rain and wind and trying to slide the hooks in order into their rack, it was after eleven o'clock and almost dark. As we got back to the ford where the mountain river cuts through the boreen we could hear that the rain had put it into flood, and the foam flashing past us in the dusk showed us the sudden speed of the water. It is not the volume of these spates that is so tricky, but their force. As I waded ahead in thigh boots, arms laden with ropes and anchors, the river tore at my legs and lifted the rocks on which I had to find balance. Ethna did not have thigh boots, but Wellingtons with pull-ups tied over them, so her crossing, when I went back to help her, was uncomfortable as well as alarming.

There's nothing so much fun, she says, as messing about by the sea.

A Day for Twins

"LIKE SHEEP," said our goatkeeper's manual, "goats seem to be able to postpone or accelerate the birth of their kids to take advantage of good weather." As a dismal start to June succeeded the wettest May since Noah, it seemed that Sally might have to put off her kidding indefinitely. Meanwhile, in case she decided to give up and do it indoors, I dug out the bedding in the shed, scrubbed the walls and floor with Dettol and spread out a bale of freshhay. This would be the first livestock birth on our homestead, and I wanted to have it right.

The average period of a goat's gestation is 150 days, and the date of Sally's visit to the puck across at Headford was written up on the blackboard in the kitchen. But the goat's normal range is from 143 days to 157 days, so there was plenty of room for wondering. On the manual's advice, I ran my hand inquisitively over the bulge in Sally's right side every morning. So long as I could feel some movement, the kidding was unlikely within twelve hours. Then, if I spotted a change in the shape of her rump, things might start to happen in three hours.

It seemed to me, towards the end, that any movement in her right side could be found just as readily in her left; the goat has four rumbling stomachs. Meanwhile, I studied the diagrams that showed what to do if one of the kids got stuck — how to push a hand into the womb and sort out heads and legs and bring the right combination into the uterus. Our local vets are 20 and 30 miles away and hardly to be counted on in an emergency. I clipped my fingernails short, but hoped these do-it-yourself obstetrics would not be necessary.

The 150th day, as it happened, dawned sunny and still. Said the manual: "The first good kidding day which comes within the fortnight in which the kids are due is the normal choice of an experienced mother. A good kidding day is a mild and humid one with a minimum of wind . . ." This was Sally's first pregnancy: would she respond to the weather? The stirrings in her bulge seemed as vague as ever. I tethered her in The Hollow, at the shady spot where the stream swerves through the hedge. It was the kind of sheltered, secluded place which a goat might choose herself, but I could keep an eye on it from where I was weeding the salsify.

And yet, after all this surveillance, she fooled me utterly! Less than fifteen minutes after I had been across the stream to feel her bulge (was there movement or wasn't there?), a couple of sharp little bleats made me look up from the weeds, then hurry incredulous, into The Hollow.

The first kid was already being licked into life; a pink balloon bobbing under Sally's tail promised another very soon. Ethna had driven to a neighbour's house, so I took a bicycle and pedalled furiously up the hill to fetch her. We arrived back in time to watch the second birth, from the first peep of the hooves to the final, plastic-wrapped tumble to the grass. Sally seemed, if anything, to welcome our attendance; she continued to graze unperturbed between the licking of her twins. We worried because the kids took so long to find her teats and seemed so inept at "plugging in".

Any farmer would have smiled at our excitement. But I have never seen any mammal born, except for kittens. The Rotunda did not ask me in, all those years ago. Now, at lambing time, the ewes are nervous of strangers and we are careful not to intrude on the yeanings taking place across the hedge. And despite broad hints to our neighbours, they have not yet remembered to send a runner to bring me to a calving. Ethna watched calves being born in her Cavan childhood, but even to her there was something affectingly special about the birth of Sally's kids.

They are a billy and a female. In some rural areas, most male kids are drowned at birth. But the Connacht population of goats (and in particular of pedigree Saanens) is still sparse enough to make that seem wasteful. At the worst, we can eat the billy at three months — but somebody else will have to kill him. The young of most species are appealing, but silky white kids are outrageously so; not for nothing did man borrow their name for his own children. At less than a week old they come butting at my Wellingtons and leap up and down from the boulder in the hen run. I find myself standing to watch them when I should be weeding or planting.

In the last chapter, I recorded our first attempts at using the spillet from the shore — how we got the line and hooks into a terrible tangle on the sand; how we let the gulls take the baits and found one hooked and drowned; how we caught a flounder and rejoiced.

For our third attempt, the spillet was reduced to a more manageable length — 50 hooks spaced out along 100 yards of line. And instead of running a rope from one of the anchors to a spar of the old wreck on the strand — which cut down the risk of losing our gear, but severely limited its range — we chose a bright orange buoy from my collection of beachcombed trawlerballs and secured it to one of the anchors on a couple of fathoms of line.

This left us free to put down the spillet where it might have most chance, We set it, at dead low tide, across the channel of the mountain river where it runs into the sea. We baited the hooks with chunks of mackerel and then, as the tide began to run up the channel, waded out into the sea and dropped anchors with the line stretched between them.

We came back at 5 a.m. next morning, just as the buoy was rolling about in the waves. But what really caught our eyes was the little flock of herring gulls swooping low above the water and mewing excitedly. Then, as I broke into a trot across the soft sand, I saw that two of the gulls were fluttering and bouncing above the surf like captive kites, hooks glittering in their beaks.

It was lucky that the gulls had only just found the line: I was able to grab the birds and extract the hooks with little more damage than a torn tongue. They flew off at once, taking their companions with them.

And we had fish! Three plaice, a turbot and two thornback skate — about a stone of fish in all. So at last we have found a key to the other half of our environment. Now there is new promise in the flood and ebb of the tide.

Horns of a Dilemma

PART OF THE winsome appearance of the new-born kid are the two tight little curls of hair on top of its head. Within a few days of birth, two little bumps can be felt at the centre of the curls. Left to themselves, these bumps soon break through the kin as cute, but sharp, little horns like those on the satyrs of mythology. Unfortunately, growing horns, like ageing satyrs, lose their cuteness. Even if never used in anger, they can catch in things — the milker's eye, for example. So, if our two kids were to fetch a proper price, they would have to be "disbudded".

In regions well settled by goatkeeping homesteaders, this would simply mean calling in the vet. There are parts of Wales, by all accounts, where a vet could spend half his time tending the Toggenburgs, Saanens and Anglo-Nubians of struggling refugees from the cities (if, that is, he was happy to be paid in cheese). But the pedigree dairy goat is still so rare in Connacht that vets have no experience in their husbandry. No one would dream of disbudding the scrub goat kept to chew back the briars or as a talisman against brucellosis. Even the disbudding of calves can be rare enough in a vet's practice: the farmer may attempt it himself, with a stick of caustic, but more commonly he calls in the vet to de-horn at a later stage.

A kid needs to be disbudded within a week of birth, before the horn takes root in the skull, so it seemed a good idea for us to learn how to do it ourselves. But we recoiled in some dismay from the advice of our goatkeeper's manual. — "The best method of disbudding kids," it said, "is the use of the red-hot disbudding iron, obtainable from veterinary suppliers. Two operators are required: one to hold the kid firmly between his knees, the other to manipulate the iron. The iron should be heated to cherry-red heat and applied briefly (six seconds) but firmly to the horn buds, searing down to the skull..." Even with the kid properly anaethetised, the book confessed, "the human operator is often in agony."

We cast around for some other way. If the stick of caustic worked on calves, should it not also work on kids? But having bought the stick and read the instructions and warnings, I began to be doubtful: to end with crumpled, twisted horns would be worse than leaving them alone. I decided to telephone an expert, a commercial goatkeeper in the Midlands. The caustic, he agreed, was not a good idea.

"What you do," he instructed helpfully, "is get yourself a piece of copper tubing, three-quarter-inch and shape a bit of wood as a handle for it. Then you stick it in the fire, and while it's heating..." He went on to detail the anaesthetising of a kid with chloroform, sprinkled on cotton wool inside a cocoa tin.

"You can't really go wrong," he insisted reassuringly. "You're an intelligent chap, good with your hands and all that. You won't burn through the skull." In thanking him, my gratitude already fought with dread.

Indeed, as I hunted for some copper tubing left over from the plumbing, and Ethna, as the pharmacist, went off to visit our patient chemist in Louisburgh, I found myself getting more and more uptight — for once, the word is exact. The more I rehearsed the scene in my mind, the more unthinkable it became.

Ethna, on the other hand, while just as humane, has a dogged, stoical streak, instilled by a Catholic childhood, that tends to surface on occasions such as this. Faced with an unpleasant solution to a problem, she will put her head down and go through with it while I am still procrastinating. In an "equal" marriage, fortunately, the male is not stuck with his *macho* role. I cannot cauterise a kid with a red-hot iron; Ethna cannot go far up ladders. We each do what we can.

Thus, as we knelt together on the kitchen floor, giving the first kid whiffs of chloroform, it was Ethna who, being the vet, was getting more tight-lipped every moment. But in the event her nerve was not to be tested. It took much longer than we expected for the chloroform to have effect: we would decide the kid was asleep, finding no resistance when we lifted a leg, and withdraw the chloroform — whereupon he would raise his head and bleat for his mother. By the time Ethna reached for the home-made disbudding iron, left heating in the range, the tubing had gone soft and collapsed. With undisguised relief we abandoned the surgery, put the kid out in the air to sleep it off and broke out a bottle of parsley wine.

In the end, the twins were disbudded by Charlie, our favourite vet from Westport, who decently took no exception to our amateur meddling (vets, unlike doctors, are not at all pompous in this regard). He disbudded the kids with a scalpel under local anaesthetic and cauterised the roots with a red-hot screwdriver to make sure. Next time, if we give him proper warning, he will probably do the job with an electric disbudding iron. I can't say the operation didn't hurt them, but they recovered with astonishing speed and were racing, helter skelter, up and down the banks of the stream.

But that was not the end to the week's humanitarian concerns. In our ventures with the spillet, we sometimes catch more seagulls than fish. The other morning, arriving to lift the line at Barnabaun, a quiet cove to the north of here, we found no fewer than seven gulls bobbing on the water, spaced out in a line like corks above a net. Five of them were drowned. The other two, as I released them from the hooks, flew off with badly-mangled beaks. Not surprisingly, we had no fish — although, back at our own channel, we have found gulls sharing the line with skate and dogfish.

The birds are a vexing problem. I am not too worried ecologically: the food thrown on the urban rubbish dumps has encouraged a population explosion among herring gulls, so that the death of a dozen a week on our spillet is neither here nor there. But it is not a fitting way for these gulls — nearly all of them in first-year plumage — to end their lives, held and dragged under as the tide rises. When I set the spillet, I wade out into the surf as far as my thigh boots permit, but still the gulls come to dive when we have gone, spotting the flash of mackerel skin in the shallow water.

If we cut off the skin, the soft chunks of fish fall apart. I have tried folding the skin inwards as I bait the hooks, but this is very slow work and not successful. An alternative is to set the line only at dusk, but this can leave us racing to beat the dark and cursing every tangled hook; it also cuts down severely on the number of tides we can fish. For all my scruples and sentiment, it may have to be a war of attrition.

Harbour Works

THERE ARE MEN — my predecessor in this house was one of them — who can handle a currach single-handed. They are not giants, as a rule, but stocky, sinewy men who shuffle seawards under that monstrous black carapace, arms spread to the gunwales, eyes popping, heart pounding. The trick, they say, is in the balance.

When I first lifted our upturned currach, hoisting the bow to prop it on my shoulder, the revelation of its weight was just appalling. Somewhere in my reading some reference to "these flimsy craft" must have set up quite the wrong expectations. A tent is flimsy, so is an airship: a thing may be flimsy and still crush you flat. That is how it feels, underneath a currach — that it is going to crush you. And if you should trip and fall, then of course it may.

I was holding up the bow on that occasion so that Joe, our neighbour, could take the lead position, burly shoulders set beneath the front seat. I crept in behind him and followed instruction, taking the weight on my back and straightening legs that seemed, on the first step forward, to have turned to rubber. The few yards down the grassy bank and across the sand to the sea were the most frightening walk of my life.

Our currach is heavier than most. Its length, about 17 feet, is fairly standard, but the Inishturk canoe is deep-bodied, with a full inner skin of laths and a strong vertical transom for an outboard engine. On the other hand, a currach is at its lightest when new, before there has been time for the sand to blow into every crevice — adding perhaps fifty pounds to the weight — and before successive tarrings have thickened the shell.

So even before it grew obvious that we could not interest any stalwart young neighbour in fishing expeditions and that Ethna and I would have to manage by ourselves, my thoughts were turning to a winch and a launch and a launching trolley. Given the apparent ease with which the men of Connacht march their canoes to the tide, it was significant that none of our neighbours raised an eyebrow at this non-traditional approach. The fact is that any man finds the currach a dire weight to carry and that any way of avoiding it makes sense. Even Joe and his neighbour Michael, who fishes with him, use a tractor to launch their canoe whenever they can.

When they arrived at the gate with a tractor one day last week it was to carry our winch on the last stage of its journey across Ireland. A friend had found it for us in a Dublin scrapyard and bought it for £30. It is a compact but massively heavy piece of machinery, of great character, which looks as if it might have spent its time bolted to the deck of a cargo steamer plying between Liverpool and Maracaibo: such, at least, is my fancy. Its gears can haul great weights in leisurely but inexorable fashion.

We heaved the winch into the tractor's transport box, together with a hundredweight of cement, a few concrete blocks, a couple of buckets, timber and nails for shuttering, and every tool we could think of. By the time we set off, with Thermos flasks and sandwiches, it had become an Expedition. Joe drove the tractor, with Michael and his young son, Thomas, perched on the transport box, while I brought up the rear on my bicycle.

There is no road to the cove where we keep the currach. The boreen expires at the channel through the strand, and a track continues from the far side across the great green lawn of the commonage behind the sandhills. After that, as the shore rises to a low, rocky cliff, even a bicycle must be abandoned. The way beyond is open only to an exceptionally adventurous tractor.

Just how adventurous became apparent as Joe mounted the slope at the end of the *duach,* and began threading his way across tumbled walls and round the lichened rocks above the shore, startling the nesting wheatears. His progress was made all the more dramatic by the roar of the great swell running in from the Atlantic, spilling terraces of foam from waves of cold, bottle-green glass. It was a day of glittering sunshine and sudden, squally showers, one of which now threatened to halt our expedition in its tracks.

The only way forward was across an outcrop of rock which sloped towards the sea. At the best of times, it would have tilted the tractor precariously, but now, wetted by a stinging downpour, the slab was greasy and treacherous. Many times, walking the shore in damp weather, I have hesitated to trust my boots on just this stretch of slate. As the tractor's front wheels slipped sideways and Michael, tense beside me, urged Joe to the lowest gear, the risk began to seem hardly worthwhile. Another greasy foot and the tractor would topple to the rocks below. Joe inched backwards, checking the slide, then tried at a steeper angle. The wheels gripped and lurched forward.

Once arrived at the spray-washed turf behind the cove, the Expedition set to work in high good humour. The siting of the winch involved fine judgment and much squinting along ropes to the edge of the sea. We found an angle which would let the currach be drawn up a smooth slope of rock to lie snug above the highest spring tide. The winch had then to be propped in position while concrete was mixed for the foundation and shovelled into the shuttering. "Lovely stuff, lovely!" it was blessed in true Connacht incantation. We hoped no curious cattle would come nudging the winch before the concrete set.

For all the surging swell and angry manes of foam, the sea at the mouth of the Killary, between us and Connemara, was far from empty. A lobster boat rocked and tossed in the lee of Inishdegil and two or three currachs, all strangers, were struggling to keep their bows to the wind. Only the chance of salmon would bring men out in currachs in such a tricky sea. We could see men standing up in one of them, and I heard Michael suck in his breath.

We watched the boat move out from the island and come close inshore to the point of rock beside us, corkscrewing in the waves. One of the crew set off in the punt to inspect a net, his orange life-jacket flashing in and out of sight as the currach rose and fell between the crests. When he returned to the boat there was a moment, between the grap and the tumble over the stern, when he almost didn't make it.

Joe and Michael used the day to impress upon me the need for prudence in using a currach in these waters. "You have no business going out on any but the fine day." I remember, too, the Inishturk men who delivered the currach urging us to buy a CB radio like their own.

But I am much more timid than anyone seems to suppose; the fine, calm day is all I ask. This being so, indeed, perhaps we should have settled for a rubber dinghy and saved everyone all this trouble.

Bridle Path

THE STRAND BELOW us gives many people a touch of agoraphobia, the fear of open spaces. Something about its vast and random expanse makes it less of a playground than a barrack square: to stroll there alone is to invite a bellow from the sky, demanding one's purpose and credentials.

So we quite understand when our young daughter, small for her age at the best of times, is overwhelmed by the sense of exposure. She cannot be lured alone to the centre of the strand, even by the drifts of little pink cowries and tiny orange fans of scallops, the size of fingernails, with which to decorate her shell-boxes. Nor is she drawn to take the pony there, and this is just as well, for while the idea of Báinin galloping at full stretch beside the waves, mane flying, hooves scattering diamond spray, must be seductive, the priority for our twelve-year-old rider is to gain full control of her mount at more modest paces.

Michele will remember this summer as the time when it all came together for herself and her pony. From the first day of the holiday, she could climb into the saddle almost at will and head off from the gate at an easy trot, unafraid of tractor, motor-bike or big red bread van. This much she had achieved very largely by her own perseverance.

We bought Báinin as an unbroken two-year-old and, knowing nothing of the schooling of horses, used pony manuals and a lot of affection to make him amenable to being ridden — I would put it no more strongly than that. Over the past two years, with occasional help from knowledgeable but busy neighbours, Michele forged a good understanding with him.

He is a robust Connemara with a young pony's spirit and stubbornness, but his nature is to trust and tolerate. He would take Michele more or less where she wanted to go, at more or less the pace she urged on him. We decided early on, and with some anguish, not to try to keep her off the roads, narrow and sometimes dangerous though they are.

The local drivers soon came to know the diminutive rider in hard hat and "hunting pink" (the brilliant top of a track suit) and most visitors have allowed her to flag them down to more considerate speeds. To meet her on the road, one would not have guessed how much of her poise was due to the mutual trust of child and pony and how little discipline she could really bring to bear.

The past week or two, however, have seen the start of real control in Michele's riding. She has headed off each morning to the foot of the mountain, where a newly-mown hayfield, small and level, provides the enclosed space that is needed for the proper schooling of a pony.

Here, directed by an experienced horsewoman, she has been weaving skill into her courage and Báinín, eyes wide with surprise, has been learning to do what is asked of him. After only a few lessons, they were changing gait on cue and cantering on a zig-zag through a slalom of hazel wands.

And now they have started jumping over poles (low poles). Michele is, of course, adamant that her goal in life is to win the Aga Khan trophy. Slowly, and sloughing off a kind of puritan prejudice, I am beginning to find this not too outrageous an ambition.

Meanwhile, Ethna and I are becoming as familiar with the strand and its tidal textures as with our own acre. In the burnished end to August, we gained even higher expectations of what we can catch on the fifty hooks of our spillet.

As we went down to set the line the other evening, the first white-billows of fine-weather fog were rolling in from the sea. The strand became more than ever a great theatrical stage, with the mist making curtains and movable walls and arches. As we crossed the sand with our buoys and anchors and the bucket of coiled line, we stepped through vivid avenues of light, long tunnels through space to the distant islands. We stretched the line on the sand and baited the hooks in a swirling, luminous limbo. It fled abruptly, admitting the dusk and the last fiery glow at the horizon. We lifted the line and carried it waist-deep into the wine-dark waves.

The next morning was fit for a travel poster: mountain behind a blue filter, sea of sapphire and viridian, islands insubstantial in a Mediterranean haze. The waves were leisurely, unzipping slow lines of lacy foam. Such a calm night ought to have brought us fish, but it seemed greedy to arrive at the sea on such a morning and expect a catch as well.

Even as I lifted the right-hand anchor and turned to wade ashore, the first two or three rays broke the surface in a flurry of white wings. More rose beyond them, like kites in the glassy green walls of the waves. There were too many to let me drag the line ashore, so that I had to unhook them one by one above the water. Most rays, and especially the thornback, are armoured with rows of curved spines, each as sharp as a falcon's talon. The only safe way to grip one is to thrust your fingers into its mouth — that deceptively comical mouth on the underside of the fish. It has curving, blubbery lips like those of a clown, but these are lined with chiton rasps and grind together with all the ferocity of a teething baby.

We had 13 rays, the biggest two feet across, and a dogfish and a plaice. We are learning to distinguish between the species of ray, all of which are intricately patterned with spots and whorls, like old-fashioned kitchen linoleum. Most of our catch were thornback, reputedly the tastiest, but some were spotted ray and one bore the dark "eyes" and yellow hieroglyphs of the cuckoo ray.

One variety we would as soon not catch is the sting ray, a tropical ray which comes inshore in late summer and autumn. The big jagged spine in its whip-like tail can penetrate even the toughest rubber waders, inflicting a serious wound. The spine also injects a venom which paralyses and makes bleeding difficult to stop.

Sting rays of up to 46½ lb have been taken by shore anglers in Wexford, and specimens up to 60 lb have been caught at Fenit Pier in County Kerry. None of our ray have come up to this size, though every setting of the spillet leaves us with missing hooks and broken, steel-cored leaders. It may be just as well we never see the fish that get away in the night.

Separate Dreams

"I'D LOVE THAT sort of life, of course, but I'm afraid poor John likes his comfort a bit too much". Thus the wife, at one corner of the party.

"I wouldn't half mind doing something of the sort, but you'd never get Deirdre to leave the shops behind". Thus the husband, confidingly, at the other side of the room.

It actually does happen sometimes and is relayed from Dublin for our amusement. It is hard to imagine that either of them means a word of it. Yet sometimes this kind of conversation isn't quite a joke. The hankering to go homesteading can take hold of one partner in a marriage with all the force of revelation, while the other is left disconcerted or alarmed. Even where the idea seems to appeal almost equally, there can be anguished differences over what is practicable. "Of course it would be wonderful, but. . .".

Most of the prospective homesteaders who call in on us are of positively glowing unanimity. Most of the wives have the capable manner that takes equality for granted. But now and then there has been a wife who seemed to say little, hanging back from her husband's enthusiasm and casting glances of what could have been dismay at the litter of improvisation, the thistles in the flowerbed, the duckshit on the path. She has asked questions, rather flatly, about doctors and schools. When we have waved goodbye and turned back from the gate, I have sometimes had to say: "I don't think that's going to work".

I'm not being sexist in concentrating on the wife. Even in these liberated days, it is not likely to be the husband who is being swept along against his will or judgement. And it is the wife, in our experience, who bears the more stressful side of the homesteading adventure. For all the brave resolutions about sharing the household chores, there is always some pressing reason why the man should be engaged in interesting and challenging work outdoors while the wife spends hours inside at the sink, preparing all those lovely fresh vegetables and coaxing the range to burn wet turf. If she has not been absolutely as enthusiastic and totally committed from the start she is sometimes going to feel very cheated.

What got me going on this was a letter from a woman whose husband is pressing hard for a switch to the homesteading life. Let's call them Helen and James. Both are professionals with separate careers in the city.

A few years ago, James bought a rundown cottage in West Donegal, which he has now restored and renovated into a very comfortable second home. "During this time", writes Helen, "he has also established very deep friendships with the local inhabitants. Indeed, we are both very fond of our neighbours. This weekend and holiday refuge has now taken a very strong hold on James, to the extent that he spends most weekends away from his home and family. You may wonder why we do not join him on his expeditions. Indeed we do on many occasions.

"However, I also enjoy having a little time to relax in my own home and to meet with my friends in the city. I must also admit I find it very tiring arriving home late on a Sunday evening when I have a very early start ahead on Monday morning. James insists on staying in Donegal as late as he possibly can."

The husband, in fact, now lives for his weekends. Helen alone keeps him in the city. "I have stressed", she says, "that I will not give up my way of life for a dream that may turn into a nightmare. I have, however, encouraged James to go himself to Donegal for a 'trial run' to see if he can establish himself into the community on a permanent basis. The talk continues, but no action".

Helen is "not against" the self-supporting life. "I just want James to be aware that it is not all plain sailing. He seems to think he can live in Donegal without having regular work of some kind. I do not think this is so"

It is hard to believe that James is really so starry-eyed as to think he can survive without any cash income: his profession demands too much common sense and clear judgment. Perhaps Helen's reference to "regular work" is the clue. "He must not only think of himself and his own needs", she writes, "but must consider my needs and more so our family's. What of medical treatment, dental treatment and education? We have a very high standard here on our owndoorstep at no cost to ourselves. Will we be treated in like fashion in West Donegal? I fear not, and these are important issues. . .To take a step sideways is one thing, to step backwards is another."

What should I say to be helpful? I could try to reassure Helen about the quality of rural education. I could tell her that we feel no qualms about relying on the basic health service and the public ward (in four years, as it happens, we have needed a doctor twice). Dental treatment might be another matter, which is why we bribe our daughter to floss her teeth every day.

But this would be beside the point. What is really at issue are the values and attitudes that underpin the homesteading drive. For us, the risks of illness are offset by the benefits of clean air, pure food and the gift of silence. We think that the freedom of a country childhood makes up for losing that highly-prized place in King's Hospital School that we booked for Michele before she was out of nappies.

Some of our convictions may well be wrong-headed, but at least we hold them in common and they have sustained us through all kinds of discomfort and inconvenience and the daunting novelty of actually spending our days together. It is simply not enough to have nothing "against" this kind of life: one has got to feel a great deal for it.

Between James, overwhelmed by his sense of place, and Helen, trying so hard to do the sensible thing, there is an abyss of intuition. I don't see any point in his trying to argue or coax her into a way of life that she has every right not to want and that certainly won't work happily in the presence of the least reluctance or misgiving.

Pro Bono Publico

The last word from Ethna . . .

THE REVENUE COMMISSIONERS' demands — two of them — arrived on Budget Day, ironically reminding us that our new way of life, regarded by some as an admirable return to basics, could be looked on as a renegation of our responsibilities as citizens. We will do very little to haul the country out of the clutches of the international bailiffs; but then we have done nothing to put it there either.

We get two demand notices because the income tax offices in Dublin and Mayo both take an interest in us. Frankly, we have been nervous of severing our connections with the Dublin office because its computer pays no attention to information we send it. It continues to assess both of our incomes from employers long gone (in Michael's case six years, in mine four) and at levels that were years out of date even when we left Dublin. We regularly send it the current data and request it to update its memory banks, but as far as the Viney byte is concerned, it has a mental block — no doubt induced by trauma resulting from our aberrations. It refuses to accept the patently ridiculous information that two of its clients have given up earning money to any relevant degree.

It crouches in Teach Earlsfort nursing its pumpkin brain and its voracious appetite, impervious to any new ideas. We have an accountant we cannot afford, who calms it occasionally with soothing words and gentle touch, but it still continues to scream periodically, "I want my Liga!". And we are afraid to ignore it in case it comes and seizes our ducks and drakes.

The Castlebar office, after tentative approaches over the past four years, is obviously about to claim its territorial rights. Now to our menagerie we can add a two-ring circus: juggling ducks and drakes in one ring and parrying an awakening lion in the other.

The truth is that we do not have any *liga* or *pabulum* for either of them. We do not earn enough cash income to reach the taxable level. The greater part of our income is in kind: we grow and catch our food, save our turf, and our recreation is our environment. We are fiscal outsiders to the Minister for Finance because we pay no income tax and, because we buy very few goods, not much of other taxes either. On the other hand, we make small claims on State finances —

the small amount of VAT which we pay would cover one children's allowance and the amount of services we use. But it is not enough for social patriots to pay their own way: if we are not to be labelled "anti-social", we should pay the way for some others as well. A family with two children and an income of £10,000 per year keeps another family with two children on social welfare.

Margaret Thatcher might approve of us, if only because we balance our own budget and make minimal demands on the State. The socialists certainly do not, although at a time of rising unemployment we bequeathed two jobs to the community and increased Gross National Product (if only they had counted it) by the produce of our small holding. But we are socially selfish about that produce — we sow, harvest, transport, store and process it ourselves. We keep all the value added; there is no Multiplier effect from it in the economy. There is, as far as we are concerned, a divider effect — the more things we do for ourselves, the less money we need.

We would be more socially responsible citizens if we gave employment to a workforce for as little as we could get away with paying them, made a fortune out of their work and paid a goodly slice to the State. We would be even better citizens if we drank, smoked and owned a fleet of high-powered cars which we changed every year. We would work as hard as we do now, but the socialists still would not like us, while Margaret Thatcher definitely would.

We are niggardly consumers: we do nothing to increase demand for the goods and services of the rest of the community. We give no boost to the Buy-Irish-and-Make-More-Jobs campaign. Replacing imported vegetable seeds by saving our own makes a job only for ourselves, with an infinitesimal reduction in the balance of payments. Social welfare recipients are better economic citizens than us, because they buy goods and services and keep others in work.

A state can afford very few of us; we can be tolerated in an industrial or developing country only for humanitarian reasons, or because we make few demands and tend to solve our own problems (although even problem-solving provides work for others). We have little part in the accumulation of the capital needed for economic development, which, as we were reminded by the Minister for Finance last week, should come from the present taxpayers, not those of the future.

This analysis of our roles as citizens could be very unsettling for two people who have always regarded themselves as socialists. (My own particular colour-band in the spectrum of the Left stood for State-control of large enterprises and utilities such as transport, communications, banking, mining; co-operative control of marketing and medium-sized enterprises; and scope for enterprise at the level of the individual). And now we find ourselves neither practising what we preached nor, indeed, preaching what we practise.

If socialists are concerned with increasing economic activity and spreading it around, then we are social saboteurs. No matter how hard we work, we do it outside the mainstream of the economic system. The smallest subsistence farmer sells cattle and sheep which provide work for the benefit of others; we consume our production.

However, we are not the total renegades that the preceding line of argument might indicate. There are good aspects to our defection from an uncongenial society. We have proven that we can live on a lot less money, and with greater satisfaction than we, or anyone else, thought possible. We have increased the productivity of one acre to the level where it provides high-quality food for one family. We have also developed a safety valve for an economy unable to employ its young people: the state could encourage more of the middle-aged, who are so inclined, into our kind of early "retirement" to make room for school-leavers. If the early retirers can support themselves, then the State gains by taking the young off social welfare. The pundits now tell us that full employment is not possible under present conditions. Our way would give the young a chance to run the economy, and they might be an improvement on the older generation.

If I needed proof that specialisation increases the general standard of living, 200 years after Adam Smith propounded the theory, then I have got it at first-hand this week. Michael and Michele have gone on a camping expedition to one of the uninhabited offshore islands, and the care of the homestead has devolved on me. My working hours have jumped from twelve to sixteen, and even at that level the weeds threaten to engulf me. The hens have taken to laying out, and I set the spillet only to catch a gull. I can hear the Revenue Commissioners' perplexity: "But why do you do it?" Why can't you give up the hard labour and return to the easy life and lovely taxable income?"

NOTES

NOTES

NOTES

NOTES

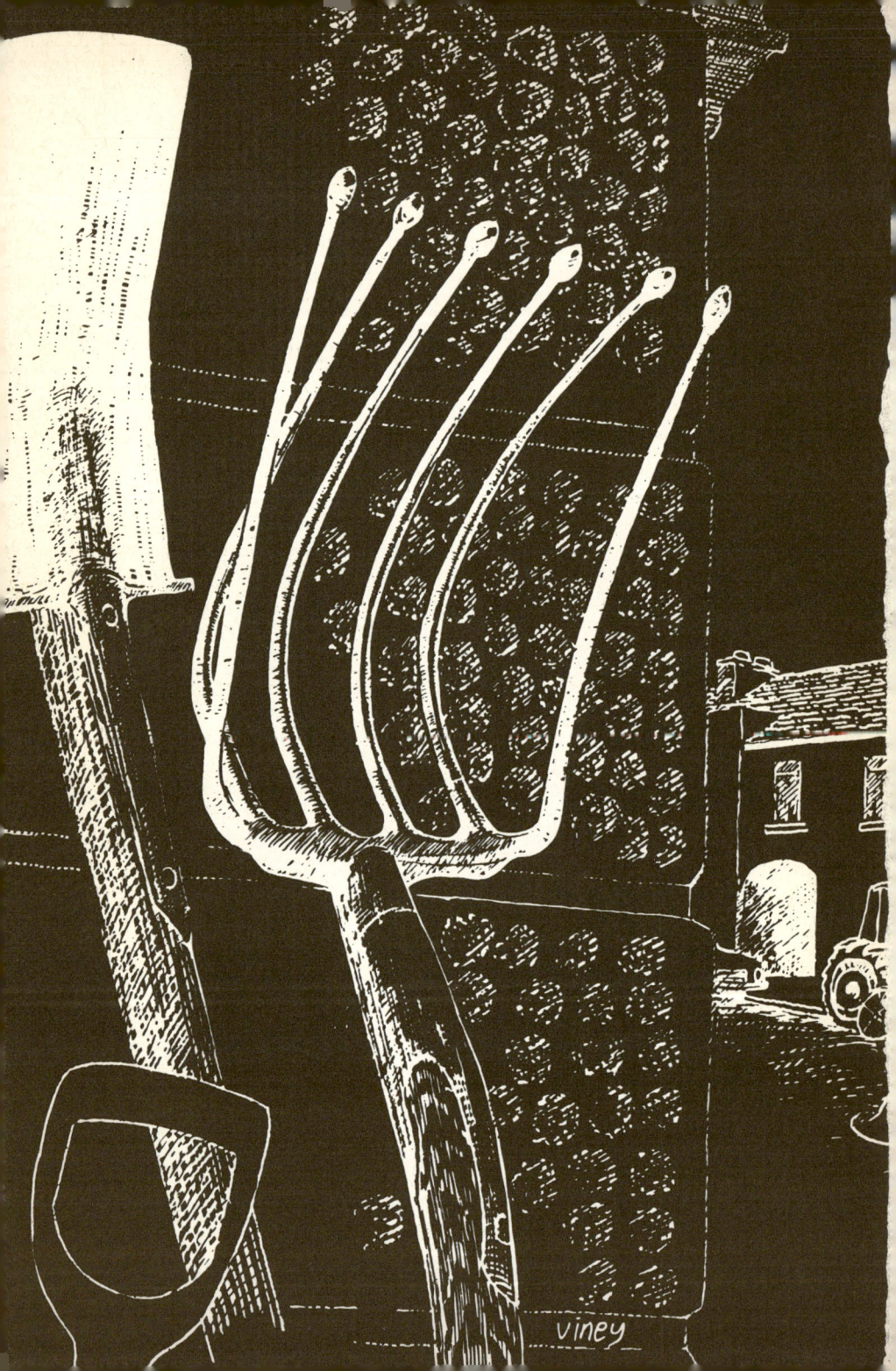